"How Can You Say That?"

Published by Pleasant Company Publications
Text copyright © 2003 by Amy Lynch

For information, address: Book Editor, Pleasant Company Publications, 8400 Fairway Place, P.O. Box 620998, Middleton, WI 53562.

Printed in the United States of America
03 04 05 06 07 08 RRD 10 9 8 7 6 5 4 3 2 1

American Girl® is a registered trademark of Pleasant Company.

Cover Photography: ibid stock photo; © Pictor International / Pictor International, Ltd. / PictureQuest
Editorial Direction: Therese Kauchak
Art Direction and Design: Susan Walsh, Lynne Wells
Production: Kendra Pulvermacher, Karn Litsheim
Credits: Excerpt on page 99 from *Raising Emotionally Intelligent Teenagers* by Maurice J. Elias, Ph.D., Steven E. Tobias, Psy.D., and Brian S. Friedlander, Ph.D., copyright © 2000 by Maurice J. Elias, Steven E. Tobias, and Brian S. Friedlander. Used by permission of Harmony Books, a division of Random House, Inc.

"How can you say that?"/ by Amy Lynch.
p. cm.
Includes index.
ISBN 1-58485-770-6
1. Interpersonal communication in children. 2. Interpersonal communication in children—Case studies. 3. Girls—Psychology.
4. Child rearing.

BF723.C57 H69 2003
153.6'0835'2—dc21   2002023972

"How Can You Say That?"

My thanks to everyone, girls and parents alike, who shared stories with me during the writing of this book. And special thanks to my husband and daughters—Phil, Sara, and Jean—who graciously allowed me to reference them on these pages. All the stories in this book are true, though the names have been changed to enhance everybody's sense of safety in their telling.

—Amy Lynch

CONTENTS

Each person's life is lived
as a series of conversations.
—*Deborah Tannen,* You Just Don't Understand

———

It is a world of words to the end of it
In which nothing solid is its solid self...
— *Wallace Stevens,* Description Without Place

Dear Parents,

Early in the 1990s, probably just about the time your daughter was born, the news about girls was not good. A national study reported that after age ten, girls' self-confidence went into steep decline. Meanwhile, researchers documented the loss of authentic "voice" (the ability to say what they really feel) among girls as they entered adolescence. The message was clear: many girls in America were at risk.

That wave of awareness, which came to be called the Girls Movement, changed things. Today's ten-year-old has grown up in an era of "girl power"—from the Spice Girls to Mulan to the Powerpuff Girls—and the press no longer routinely describes girls as "at risk." In fact, the pendulum has swung so far that, as I write this, the best-selling books about girls cast them not as victims but as villains. *Queen Bees and Wannabes, Odd Girl Out,* and *The Secret Life of Girls* all explore how mean girls can be and why. And those books, just like the reports of a decade ago, are true, too. The girls in our lives are complex people who inevitably struggle with "voice"—that critical ability to find words that honestly say who they are, what they need, and what they feel. And, as their parents, we struggle with words, too.

That's why *"How Can You Say That?"* is in your hands. We all blow it sometimes. In moments of frustration, we say words we wish we could take back. With that in mind, American Girl collected stories from more than 300 girls about words they wish they'd never said to us parents, and words they wish we hadn't said in return.

You'll find those stories, in the voices of the girls who told them, throughout this book. They are dramatic, full of relish and sometimes urgency. As I interviewed parents, I heard equal urgency. Each of us carries these conversations around in our heads. We examine them when we're alone and tell them to our friends—what we said, what she said, what it meant. Words matter.

Throughout this book you'll find scenarios in which hard words are said by a parent, by a girl, or by both. After each scenario, we offer thoughts about why this kind of exchange happens. Then there's a section called "What If You Said . . ." That's the good stuff. These sample responses are for all of us who find ourselves wishing we could snatch back the words we just said to our daughters. In that moment of regret lies opportunity. If, as you draw your breath to speak again, you can use words like those in "What If You Said . . . ," you'll be teaching "voice" at its best. You'll be able to step back from the fire, even when the girl across from you is still pouring on the gasoline.

But that is just the first step. The next is up to you, because you are the real expert when it comes to talking to your daughter. You're the one who knows her heart best. My hope, and the hope of the editors at American Girl, is that *"How Can You Say That?"* will help all us parents move through our anger to love—and give that love voice.

Girls and Words

*Why are girls so adept with words
and vulnerable to their power? And what does
that imply for us as parents?*

---

*Once I told my parents I would go for a week
without speaking to settle a problem, but it made
everything worse. I realized I couldn't survive
without talking to them.*

—Kloie, age 12

*One time Lia was caught shoplifting. I was away at the
time, and I got a phone call from her mom. Fortunately
I had the day to calm down before calling Lia that night.
When she answered the phone, I honestly still didn't know
what I would say. When she heard my voice, she said,
"Hi, it's me," and we both cried awhile. Then I said,
"There is nothing in this world that you can do that can
make me stop loving you." And that was basically it.
That was the phone call. I'm still not sure where
those words came from, but they were exactly what we
both needed right then.*

—Dan, father of a 15-year-old girl

How do girls know we love them? How do they know we really "see" them? The answer, like parenting itself, is complicated and simple at the same time. It centers on words.

There are lots of clichés, few of them flattering, about how much girls and women talk. But girls do tend to be adept with words, especially at home and in private settings. They understand the power of saying things aloud to people who matter to them. Indeed, girls use words to build one of the most important components of their lives—relationships. Years ago, I worked as a dorm mother in a school in Bolivia. One of the Spanish phrases I learned almost instantly was *me dijo*, which means "she said to me." The girls talked constantly about what one of them had said to another. The words themselves—whether affectionate or challenging— were news. They were worth talking about. A lot.

Was your daughter born to talk? Science seems to say "yes." Just because they're female, our daughters have brains that are wired for language facility, and it shows up early, when they're still in the crib. In the United States, infant girls babble more and begin to speak earlier than boys, and as girls grow up, they use longer sentences and more complex grammatical constructions than boys do. Our daughters are three times less likely to stutter than our sons are, and they're less likely to have learning disabilities related to language. By age 12, girls excel at grammar, punctuation, and

reading. Girls tend to be fluent, rattling off tongue twisters and list-
ing synonyms more quickly than boys do. Between 1960 and 1990,
psychologists surveyed 130,000 American boys and girls ages 13
to 22. In all three decades, the girls excelled in language skills.[1]

This girl-to-word link is, of course, a generalization, and your
daughter may be a quiet kid while her brother is a talker. In fact,
differences in all kinds of abilities tend to be more pronounced
within each gender than between them. Yet, again and again
researchers find that girls have innate and powerful connections to
words. Even hormones appear to play a role.

As they approach puberty, our daughters experience hormonal
surges as early as ages seven or eight. Recent research has linked
estrogen with building dendritic spines on the brain's nerve cells,
increasing the number of links and the flow of information between
neurons. At times when her estrogen level is high, your daughter
finds it easier to pronounce words, to remember what has been
said, and to find the right word quickly.[2] Her sudden facility with
puns or her rapid-fire comeback to you over dinner may be aug-
mented by estrogen surging through her system and multiplying
the linguistic highways in her brain. Even she may be surprised by
the speed with which words come to her tongue. That was the case
in the story from this mother:

1. Summarized by Helen Fisher, *The First Sex: The Natural Talents of Women and
How They Are Changing the World* (New York: Random House, 1999). Original
research was done by Judith Hall, *Nonverbal Sex Differences* (Baltimore: Johns
Hopkins University Press, 1984) and Diane Halpern, *Sex Differences in Cognitive
Abilities* (Mahwah, NJ: Lawrence Erlbaum and Associates, 1992).

2. Elizabeth Hampson, "Estrogen-Related Variations in Human Spatial and
Articulatory-motor Skills," *Psychoneuroendocrinology* 15, no. 2 (1990): 97–111.

The other night I tucked Ariel into bed and, as I turned to leave, she said in this singsong voice, "So sad to see you. Wouldn't want to be you." I'm ashamed to say this, but it irritated me and I turned around and said, "Wouldn't want to be you, either." Instantly I felt bad about that, but I went on to my room. A few minutes later, Ariel peeked in the door and said, "Can we have a 'do-over'?" And I gave her a big hug and said, "Yes, of course we can." It was the first time she had openly challenged me like that, and I think it shocked us both!

—Susan, mother of an eight-year-old girl

If your daughter is a particularly "mouthy" girl, prone to talking back, it may help you to know that it doesn't work to try to keep up with her in this area. As they grow, girls are more or less poised to sprint ahead of us in verbal races. They're also growing up in a world that is, for the most part, harsher than the one in which you and I grew up. Language in general is meaner than it used to be. Just like the rest of us, girls are influenced by what they hear at school, on TV, and on the street. As a result, parents have to make careful decisions about when to engage and when to step away, and we'll talk more about that throughout this book. Fortunately, your daughter will develop more control and good judgment with this overwhelming flow of words as she gets older. In the meantime, you may need to lay in a substantial supply of patience.

Words Connect Us

Not only are our daughters adept at using words; they are skilled relationship builders, too—and that makes words even more important to them. Psychologists confirm what attentive parents have always known—that from a very young age, a girl identifies herself as an individual who, like the hub of a wheel, exists at the center of a complex set of relationships. When a girl's relationships are disrupted, balance and wholeness are missing. Her identity is threatened; she feels as if she's not who she thought she was. The daughter who throws herself into your arms and sobs over her betrayal by a friend is shaken to her very core. And the tools she'll use to repair the damage done will most likely be words. Conversation is essential to our daughters. It builds relationships and keeps them intact.

That's why an angry girl is more likely to give you the silent treatment than her brother is. It's often the most powerful tool she can think of to sever a tie and make her point. Of course, boys use words to build relationships too, but not to the degree girls do. Whereas boys form bonds with activity, girls get close by talking.

Words have the power to make or break our relationships with our daughters. They are the glue that binds us together, and, when misused, they drive a wedge between us.

> *Once I asked my mom something, and she said, "Just go away and leave me alone!" It hurt me, but later she apologized and I felt loved again.*
>
> —*Tylesa, age 12*

Tylesa didn't just feel relieved or okay. She felt loved again and, therefore, complete. Her mother's words had the power to drive her away and the power to mend what was broken.

Words are never wasted on our daughters. Our girls cannot help but hear us, and, of course, we hear them, too. All the words a girl speaks to you, whether muttered under her breath or yelled from deep in her lungs—the loving words and the criticism, her demands, and even her whining—are attempts to engage, attempts to be heard. As long as her words are flowing, she is trying to connect. It isn't always easy to see a girl's words that way. But if you and I reflect on what we're doing as parents when we nag, correct, or criticize our daughters, it helps us understand this dynamic. We're just trying to be heard, too—just trying to connect.

One dad whom I interviewed reflected on how words connect us when he talked about yelling at his daughter in the mornings when he was anxious to get her moving and off to school:

> *I put on my father's grim visage and assume the role I think I'm supposed to take. Sophie, though, doesn't give in. She yells back, "Don't have a cow, Dad!" I have wondered about moments like this when my daughter and I assume roles that are, perhaps, stereotypical. I have to confess there's a certain amount of comfort in doing so—a sort of affirmation that, yes, I am the father and she is my daughter, and this is how we are.*
>
> *—Joel, father of a 13-year-old girl*

In all their guises, words connect. Words get us into trouble with each other, but they are also pathways back into loving relationships. Girls are generally adroit with words—and particularly vulnerable to them, too. That means words are often the best tool you have for staying close to your daughter. She hears your words of comfort, affection, and support. Even when those words are fumbling or awkward, they fly straight to her heart.

"WOULD YOU LISTEN FOR A SECOND?"

Girl: *. . . and in my room I found this shirt, and so I know Kimmy was in there. I told her never to come in. I mean, she won't let me come in her room. She goes off on me and yells if I go in there, especially when my friends are over. But I know she came in my room because all this stuff was moved. I think she was looking through my drawers—*

Dad: *Can I say something?*

Girl: *Sure. I want to know how you're going to fix this. I cannot— cannot—have her in my room. I mean it. It's . . .*

Dad: *Just slow down. I'm going to talk to Kimmy—*

Girl: *Good, because I really mean it this time. I want a lock on my door. I know you won't let me have one, but my room is my room and not hers—*

Dad: *Hey, would you listen to me for a second?*

Girl: *Of course. What is your problem?*

What Just Happened?

Because our daughters are so very able with words, sometimes we feel as if they aren't listening to us. Once a girl discovers her talent to express herself verbally, she can become like a running faucet that's hard to turn off. She'll get over this eventually, but in the meantime it can be a problem, especially for dads, who can find it hard to tolerate a girl's continual stream of words in which a lot is said but little information is conveyed. And we don't dare tune our daughters out. We might miss something vital.

It may reassure you to know that your daughter might welcome interjections from you, as long as they're on the subject.

Researchers have found that girls are less likely than boys to end speaking by actually falling silent. Sometimes when girls have said all they want to say, they just start repeating themselves, and that's an invitation for us to begin speaking.

What If You Said . . .

A comment like "Hey, can I just get a word in here" may feel like an attack to your daughter and put her on the defensive. If you're in a situation like this, you might try words like these:

I'm having trouble knowing what you need right now. Do you want me just to listen, or do you want me to come up with solutions?

Sometimes I don't answer you because I don't want to interrupt while you're still talking.

This is confusing to me. You seem to need me to say something, even though you're still talking.

I have to admit that sometimes I have trouble paying complete attention if you talk for a long time. So I need you to tell me if something is really important to you.

"I'M SICK OF ARGUING WITH YOU"

Mom: *I think we'll go by the dry cleaners first, and then we can go on to the grocery.*

Girl: *But the grocery is closer.*

Mom: *I know, but this way the food stays cold longer.*

Girl: *I hate sitting in traffic. Let's go to the closest place first.*

Mom: *I'm sick of arguing with you. You'd argue if I said it was Thursday.*

Girl: *Well, it's Friday, so there!*

What Just Happened?

Sometimes some girls seem determined to argue with us. If this is the case at your house, keep in mind that your daughter uses words like lifelines, casting them out into the water to see who'll take hold. If she's constantly arguing with you, she is "casting," attempting to connect, perhaps to let you know that she is changing. Her cognitive abilities may have just taken a giant leap forward, as happens during puberty and adolescence. **Maybe she doesn't quite know what to do with her new ability to reason (and to argue), but she needs you to notice and validate it.** That's likely the case in this story, told to me by a mom who saw the humor in it:

> *I went to a talk about kids by a therapist. He said that adolescents have this new mental ability and so forth and they have to prove who they are, and so they argue. I went home and my daughter asked what the lecture had been about. I told her and she said, "That's not true. I argue with you because you're wrong."*
>
> —*Dorothy, mother of an 11-year-old girl*

Psychologist Terri Apter, who wrote *Altered Loves* (New York: Fawcett Books, 1991), a landmark study of mothers and daughters, concluded that girls who argue with their moms aren't so much trying to separate as they are trying to stay close. They're using arguments to renegotiate the relationship. Roni Cohen-Sandler came to the same conclusion when she researched mother-daughter conflict for *"I'm Not Mad, I Just Hate You!"* (New York: Penguin Putnam, 2000). Odd as it sounds and contrary as it feels, sometimes girls use arguing as a way of making sure they're still connected to us.

What If You Said . . .

If your daughter seems determined to argue, keep in mind that this, too, shall pass. She will grow older and figure out more productive ways of relating to you. In the meantime, remove yourself from the situation when you need to, and try commenting on the act of arguing itself rather than the subject she is arguing about.

I hear you. I know you want to go to the cleaners first. Give me a minute to think it through.

I don't mind when you argue with me if you're not being disrespectful of me. Can you tell the difference?

You're really good at arguing. But is this worth arguing about?

I don't like arguing with you. It makes me feel frustrated and tired. How does it make you feel?

You know, lots of girls and parents go through stages where they feel like arguing a lot. It usually means the girl is changing. Do you think that's true for you?

"SHUT UP!"

Girl: *Mom, I need my allowance. You said I'd get it on Saturday, and it's Monday already.*

Mom: *You didn't take out the garbage. And you know the deal—no allowance until your chores are done.*

Girl: *That's not fair. I had too much to do this week! You know how busy I was. Besides, my allowance is my money!*

Mom: *You need to remember to do your chores first. Why can't you do that?*

Girl: *You always nag me! Shut up and just leave me alone!*

What Just Happened?

Our daughters use "shut up" with their friends as a casual comeback that means "You've got to be kidding." So if your daughter says "shut up" to you, you may have to listen to her tone and look at her body language to know the intent behind her words.

However, in the scenario above, the girl's intent is clearly disrespectful and abrasive. In that case, her words tell us a lot about how she is feeling. It translates to "I'm overwhelmed" or "It's hard for me to hear this right now" or "That's not information I can deal with." "Shut up" is her attempt to put up a temporary protective barrier to what she does not want, or cannot bear, to hear you say.

It's worth noting that families are all over the map with this phrase. Some families, and some parents, tolerate it more easily than others. If you find it offensive, react immediately when your daughter says it, especially if she's young and this sort of exchange is not yet a pattern between you. The best course is to give her gentle but firm directions such as, "Tell me again, this time without hurting my feelings."

The Parental "Shut Up"

If you and I use "shut up" with our daughters, the words take on a decidedly darker tone than when girls use the words with us. That's because parents are always in the "power up" position with girls. We have more power than they do. When we say "shut up," the words have an authority our daughters simply cannot muster yet because they are still children. Beyond that, "shut up" stops, or tries to stop, the flow of words and, therefore, cuts off connection. To our daughters, "shut up" from us reads, "I don't want to hear you" and, by extension, "You don't matter to me." In most cases, these words require us to apologize.

What If You Said . . .

If your daughter tells you to "shut up" in an offensive way, you might say:

That was disrespectful. Let's both stop for a minute and gather our thoughts.

I know lots of people say "shut up" to each other, but we don't do that in our family.

I need to hear an apology for what you just said.

I know you say that to your friends, but please don't say it to me.

If you can tell me how you feel without being rude, it will be a lot easier for me to hear you.

"DAD! WOULD YOU JUST LISTEN TO ME?"

Girl: *So anyway, Katie has this thing about me wearing this top, the same one she has, and—*

Dad: *Hand me that plate, will you?*

Girl: *Huh? Here. And I don't know what to do because every time I wear it, she makes this scene. She's like, "You wore it again," and I'm like, "Yeah, so—"*

Dad: *I want to talk to you about the fact that you didn't clear the table last night, even though it was your turn.*

Girl: *I'm sorry, I forgot. Anyway, so Katie says in front of everybody that she's going to throw away her top, and that made me really mad, but Jess said—*

Dad: *Will you get the spinach out of the fridge?*

Girl: *DAD! Would you just listen to me? It won't hurt you to wait one second while I tell you something!*

Dad: *And it won't hurt you to show some respect! Go to your room!*

What Just Happened?

Girls use words to connect with us. If we interrupt them with contradictions or comments that show we aren't listening, they feel rejected and ignored. True, the girl in the example above wasn't talking about anything earthshaking, but to most girls most of the time, that's not the point. The very fact that she was telling her dad about her day meant she was inviting him to relate. She felt cut off and discounted when he didn't listen.

Daughters absolutely yearn to be acknowledged by their parents. Your attention turned her way fills a deep and powerful need inside your daughter—a need nobody else can fill as you do. That's why she needs to know you're listening. Reject her words, and she feels as if you're rejecting her.

Interruptions vs. Overlap

Interruptions are different from *overlap*, which means talking over another person but with comments that are supportive or add to what the other person is saying. Researchers find that girls tend to be comfortable with overlap. Just listen to any group of girls talking, and you'll hear lots of it. If the dad in our example had interjected, "You mean Katie got mad about that?" his daughter would have heard that as supportive overlap rather than an interruption.

What If You Said . . .

If your daughter catches you interrupting, slow down and establish eye contact. If you need to, set parameters that let her know you'll gladly listen later. In the meantime you might say:

You have my attention now, but I wish you'd found some other way to get it. Can we talk about what just happened?

I'm sorry I was interrupting you, but as you can see, now isn't a good time for me to talk. Can you tell me the whole story after I finish what I'm doing?

I was interrupting you, and that never feels good. I'm sorry. I want to hear your story. I just can't hear it right now.

THE SILENT TREATMENT

Girl: *You told the Johnsons I couldn't go to OctoberFest with them, and you didn't even talk to me about it! That's not fair!*

Mom: *It was a little thing. I knew you were busy, and I didn't know you wanted to go so badly.*

Girl: *That's not the point. You try to run my whole life! This happens all the time!*

Mom: *Why are you getting so upset?*

Girl: *(no answer)*

Mom: *I'm talking to you. Hello?*

Girl: *(no answer, stomps off to her room)*

Mom: *Fine. I could use a little quiet for a change.*

What Just Happened?

Words are powerful in our daughters' lives, and silence is equally powerful. A daughter who refuses to speak to us is attempting to withdraw from connection, to make her feelings unavailable to us. This gives her a sense of power and control. But the girls who shared their stories with us reported that not talking to their parents was hard. "I said I wouldn't talk to my family ever again. But that afternoon, I couldn't stand it any longer," one girl wrote. She felt compelled to talk, because her ongoing connection to her parents is vital to her sense of self. At some level, our daughters feel bereft if their relationships with us are disrupted—even when they're the ones who break off the daily give-and-take.

Truth be told, we feel bereft, too, down deep. Yet our surface emotion may be anger, and understandably so. We put a lot of work into parenting, and in doing so, we allow ourselves to become vulnerable—as we should; after all, that is the nature of love. Therefore, a girl's intentional silence has the power to sting.

A good question to ask when faced with the silent treatment is "What do I want?" The answer, of course, is that you want the relationship restored—you want everybody talking again, and civilly. It follows that civility is your best tool. Be careful not to say, "Fine. I just won't talk to you either." That only gives your daughter's actions more power, assuring her that she has found a weapon that really gets under your skin and causes you to abandon your role as adult and to act like a hurt child yourself. Usually the best way to reach your goal is to let your daughter know that you're available and (this is essential) that you are not overly afraid of or upset by her silence. Your quiet confidence in the longtime love between you will create a safe space into which her words, in time, can flow.

What If You Said . . .

If your daughter stops talking to you, look for words that let her know your love is stronger than the silence that threatens to cut you off.

I can understand that you don't want to talk to me right now. That's normal sometimes between girls and parents.

I know you aren't talking to me these days, and I can respect that. But I'm still here, honey. I always will be.

When you're ready to talk again, I have lots to tell you.

I miss it when we don't talk.

"DON'T YOU EVEN KNOW WHO I AM?"

Mom: *Okay, everybody. Let's get moving. Got your backpack, Ali? Don't forget your lunch.*

Beth: *Mom, I'm Beth. You called me Ali again.*

Mom: *Did I? Mornings are such a rush. (calling up the stairs) Ali, time to go!*

Beth: *Aren't you even going to say you're sorry?*

Mom: *It was an accident, Beth.*

Beth: *But you should apologize! You do that all the time. Don't you even know who I am?*

What Just Happened?

A girl's name is made of the most important words in the world to her—it *is* her! If you are a mom, you probably remember making up a "dream" name for yourself when you were eight or ten years old. Most girls do. A dream name is a name you wished you had because it was, you thought, more dramatic, more interesting, more *you*. (Personally, I wanted Amanda Janice, with an accent on Ja-NEESE, of course, rather than plain old Amy Jane.) Because girls attach so much identity to their names, they are awfully sensitive to being called by somebody else's.

A girl's primary developmental task at this age is to figure out who she is as a genuinely mysterious and completely unique person. She is constantly learning new things about how she feels and what she is capable of doing, and she depends on you and me to notice this emerging sense of identity. If we accidentally call her by the wrong name, especially when we're busy and have so much on our minds, it may seem like a small enough thing to you and me.

But a girl is likely to feel the slight at a deeper level than we realize. To her, our calling her by the wrong name can indicate that we aren't paying attention to her, that we don't really "see" her and recognize the person she is.

The specific misspoken name we use has an effect, too. If I call my daughter by her sister's or her cousin's name, she is going to draw some sort of conclusion based on the person I confused her with. She's going to ask herself, "Am I like that person? Is that why Mom said her name instead of mine?" She may assume that I'm comparing her to her sister or cousin or that I wish she were like one of them. And if I call her by the name of someone she doesn't like or feels superior to, then she is really going to feel insulted. This simple mistake can get awfully complicated.

What If You Said . . .

If you called your daughter by somebody else's name, words like these may help:

I can't believe I called you by the wrong name. You're my one and only Beth, and there's nobody like you in the world.

I'll try not to do that again, but sometimes my old brain is going to slip a bit. Keep reminding me, okay?

My mom used to do that to me, too. It made me feel like she didn't notice me. I'm sorry if it makes you feel that way.

"WHY ARE YOU SO SENSITIVE?"

Girl: *If I sweep the sidewalk, can I go over to Lizzy's? What are you doing to the lawnmower?*

Dad: *Trying to see if there's gas in the tank. Move over, please. You're in my light.*

Girl: *Okay! Sure! No problem! You never want me around!*

Dad: *What? Why are you blowing up all of a sudden? Why are you so sensitive?*

What Just Happened?

All of us size up a person's message by listening to the cadence, the lilt, and the inflection of the words, but girls seem to go through stages when they're especially sensitive to the way words are spoken. Your daughter probably started developing this ability in infancy. As a group, baby girls listen more intently to music and pay closer attention to people's voices. During recent years, scientists have examined brain scans of men and women and have concluded that women use more parts of their brains when they're listening than men do. If your daughter's typical, her language centers are spread broadly and connected to several areas in her brain. That means she makes myriad associations when she listens to your words, extracting lots of meaning from what she hears.[3]

In the scenario above, for example, the girl took offense not at what the dad said—which was basically harmless—but at how he said it. Our daughters overreact sometimes because they hear messages that we don't mean to send.

3. Helen Fisher, *The First Sex: The Natural Talents of Women and How They Are Changing the World* (New York: Random House, 1999).

What If You Said . . .

If your daughter seems upset by how you've said something, try words like these:

I'm not sure why you're upset. Can you explain what you thought I just said?

I know that sometimes I speak gruffly. I'm sorry if that makes you think I'm angry with you or that I don't love you.

When you react so quickly, I have trouble knowing what to say. Can we start this conversation over and try to figure out what went wrong?

Words and Self-Confidence

Just as words can tear down a girl's spirit, they can also build it up. For her book *Everyday Ways for Raising Smart, Strong, Confident Girls* (New York: St. Martin's Griffin, 1999), Barbara Littman surveyed high school and college girls around the country about what their parents did to build their strength and confidence. Again and again, the answer was the same: "Tell her she's beautiful. Tell her you cherish her." Affirming words from parents were essential, the girls said. Among the words the girls liked best were *neat, interesting, wonderful,* and *radiant.* "Girls need to know they are accepted just the way they are, flaws and all," Littman concluded. "A parent who communicates this has a good chance of raising a girl who, as a young woman, will be self-confident."

"DON'T TAKE THAT TONE WITH ME"

Mom: *I forgot to pick up your band uniform at the cleaners.*

Girl: *Great. Now I have to go to practice without it, and we're supposed to dress out.*

Mom: *(checking her planner) Maybe I could leave work and get it at lunch tomorrow.*

Girl: *(sarcastically) Right. That'll fix everything.*

Mom: *Don't take that tone with me, young lady!*

What Just Happened?

Sometimes it's not what she says but how she says it. A girl between the ages of 8 and 14 is developing verbal skills in great leaps and bounds. There's new vocabulary, new syntax, and an ability to create and follow verbal logic. Then there's tone. We know that girls tend to "hear" lots that isn't actually said, gathering information from the speaker's body language and from the way someone's voice is pitched or modulated. Girls learn how to send those signals, too.

Our daughters develop this skill in part because they're dealing with very complex and competitive situations with peers at school. Even today, most girls hesitate to express anger or dislike for someone forthrightly; they usually communicate such emotions in sly and indirect ways—with a sneer, a glance to one side, or the tiniest note of falseness in the voice. In short, anger and competition subverted become meanness, and girls caught up in schoolgirl interactions sometimes become experts at using an ice-cold timbre. This is explored in detail in Rachel Simmons's *Odd Girl Out: The Hidden Culture of Aggression in Girls* (New York: Harcourt Trade, 2002).

This unfortunate expertise comes home to visit us, too. Your best course is usually to let your daughter know that you see what she's doing and remind her, when you can, that you are not the enemy.

What If You Said . . .

When your daughter uses a tone with you that is sneering or cold, you might say:

You communicate a lot with your tone, and I can hear it.

If you feel angry, say so directly. Tell me how you feel, but don't play games with your voice.

I know it's useful for you to be able to talk that way to someone who might be trying to hurt you. But it's a tone that doesn't serve a purpose between you and me.

I try to keep my tone respectful when I talk with you, and I appreciate your doing the same.

When She's Rude

Every girl should be assertive (able to voice what she feels and what she needs) but not rude (thoughtlessly or needlessly hurtful). How can you teach your daughter the difference? Think of yourself as an assertiveness coach, and when she's rude, use words like these:

"Think about the difference between being cruel and being clear. Then try again."

"What do you really want to happen next? What kind of words will get that result?"

"If you can say what you need to say without being so hurtful, I'll be more likely to understand your point."

"YOU LIED TO ME!"

Girl: *I can't wait to go to the parade this Saturday.*

Dad: *I need to talk with you about that. I know we planned to go, but some things are changing for me at work, and I can't promise that I'll be able to take you after all. It all depends on what happens at work tomorrow. I'll do my best.*

Girl: *But you said you'd take me.*

Dad: *And I will if I can. I just can't be sure right now.*

Girl: *No fair! You lied to me!*

Dad: *It was not a lie! Don't accuse me of lying.*

What Just Happened?

Sometimes, during the elementary school years when girls are struggling to assert control over their schedules, they accuse us of lying to them when, in fact, our plans simply changed.

If we step into a girl's shoes for a moment, we can see that a change in a schedule she was depending on feels like a lie or a betrayal to her, not just a disappointment. Deep down, she longs to believe that we have complete power over our lives (because that would make her feel completely safe and secure).

"White" lies upset our daughters, too. The year my daughter Sara was nine, I took a vase given to me for my birthday, rewrapped it, and gave it to a friend for her birthday. When Sara saw my friend open her gift, she yelled, "You got that for your birthday, and you said you really liked it!" What a moment! Embarrassed, I tried to laugh off the situation, as did my gracious friend. But Sara continued to insist that I had lied. She was telling the truth as she knew it. Later I learned that behavior like this is a stage of cognitive/social development that girls go through around age eight or nine.

Carol Gilligan calls this behavior "whistle blowing" in her book about girls and adolescence, *Meeting at the Crossroads* (Ballantine Publishing Group, 1993). During this developmental stage, a girl still thinks concretely and absolutely. To her, the truth is the truth and a lie is a lie—and that's that. In coming years she'll comprehend the subtle area of white lies or omission.

Finally, we know that for girls, words more or less equal relationship. If the words are false, then a girl concludes the relationship is untrustworthy, too. That's another reason she reacts violently if she feels we have lied. She fears for the relationship.

What If You Said . . .

If your school-age daughter accuses you of lying when the circumstances were beyond your control, try these words:

I hear you. I can see that it felt awful to you when I told you I might not be able to go. It felt like a lie, even though I try to tell you the truth always.

I can see why you feel I lied. I want you to know that I do my very best not to promise you things I can't deliver on later. It's just that sometimes my work schedule changes.

I can see the truth is important to you. It's important to me, too. And I can see you feel hurt because I had to change the plans. Let's talk about some back-up plans so that we can spend some time together this weekend, no matter what.

I'm glad you're so aware of what's true and what's a lie. That's an important thing to understand. I hope you'll also understand that I did not mean to lie to you.

When Words Hurt

How can you put the brakes on emotions so that your words calm your daughter instead of inciting her?

Once I said the traditional "I hate you" to my mom.
Later I apologized, but I meant it at the time.

—BBallGal, age 11

I was so irritated with her that I lost it and yelled, "You're
an ungrateful brat! Go ahead and run away.
See if I care!" That was a terrible day.

—Kathy, mother of a 13-year-old girl

This chapter is for all of us who've ever found ourselves standing alone in that sudden, awful silence immediately after an exchange of angry words with a girl who means the world to us. (Listen—is that the door to her room slamming?) It's a little like standing on air, that moment, a little like waiting to fall. All of us who parent girls have spent some time in that space of disconnection and hurt that I call the "after moment." If our emotions get out of the way long enough to let us think just then, the first words that race to the surface are usually, "What the heck just happened?!!?" We replay the event in our minds, wishing that we hadn't said what we said or that our daughter hadn't said what *she* said—or both. We wonder if we could have brought the conversation to a more amicable ending. Could we have said anything that would have fostered connection instead of confrontation?

Rest assured that if you're in that moment now or have visited the land of regret recently, you're not alone. (That's me over there to your right.) I've always been surprised when perfectly wonderful, caring parents confess remorse over hard words they've exchanged with their daughters. And I'm just as surprised when girls I know to be terrific kids admit that they've screamed unimaginable things at their parents. We absolutely ache to stay close to our daughters, and they yearn to connect with us, so why do things go wrong? Why do we all blow it sometimes?

Denying Our Deepest Feelings

We make a mess of things because we're human—we and our daughters both. Harsh words spring up because the connections between our daughters and ourselves are so intense—because we care so much and worry so much, and because it is a fearful thing to be this closely connected to anybody else in the world. These are not subtle feelings. Naturally, they're hard to express, hard to manage. **That's our first clue to recognizing and avoiding words that hurt: destructive words almost always deny or distort what we're feeling down deep.**

By destructive language I mean yelling, name-calling, dissing, exaggerating, criticizing, employing the silent treatment, snipping, verbal ambushes, attacking, blaming, sarcasm, and nearly all teasing. Whoever said "Sticks and stones may break my bones, but words will never hurt me" forgot what it was like to be a child and never parented a girl.

Sarcasm is a handy example of distorted expressions of our deepest feelings.

> *Once I was fighting with my parents and I said, "Thanks for making my life a living hell!" Later I realized how much that must have hurt.*
>
> *—Lapio, age 12*

On the parental front, I've said, "Thanks for being so helpful" to my daughters when they've managed to not lift a hand while I've cleaned the house alone. Both of these sarcastic statements shield or distort what the speaker is really feeling.

Lapio was feeling angry and frustrated with her parents, perhaps for very good reasons, but she didn't articulate that. And as for me, the next time I'm pushing the vacuum cleaner around while one of my daughters lies on the couch reading a novel, I hope I'll have the presence of mind to turn off the machine, go get myself a cup of coffee, come back, sit down, and say something like, "You know, I feel really unappreciated when . . ." Then I'll be talking about what I feel. I may even be able to talk about my hopes for my daughter's behavior, instead of responding to my fears that I'm raising an ungrateful child and that I'll still be vacuuming, all alone, this time next year. Saying what I really feel is hard, though. It's easier just to take my sarcastic shot and keep vacuuming. Being a grown-up is definitely a challenge.

When You Attack Back

When your daughter attacks your relationship, screaming "I hate you!" or "I wish you weren't my dad," it hurts—terribly. What if you cave in, get angry, and return the attack? This is probably a case in which you should find someone outside the family to talk with about your anger.

Attacking the relationship is a verbal tactic that is always and forever off-limits to us parents. There simply aren't any circumstances when it's okay to say "I wish you weren't my daughter" or "I hate you, too." Simply because we always have more power than our daughters do, they rely on *us* to sustain the connection between daughter and parent. Besides, the connection itself is part of who our daughters understand themselves to be. To them, an attack on the relationship is, in effect, a direct attack on them.

Finally, our daughters may not necessarily remember their own attacks, but because their dependence on us is so profound and deep, they do remember every word we say if we attack or deny our connections to them.

Navigating Our Emotions

Parenting is like piloting a plane. It's our job to get the passengers—in this case, our daughters—safely to their destination. We have to stay calm, because if we panic, it excites the passengers, and this lot is pretty excitable to begin with.

Girls have a reputation for being emotional, and there is some basis for that generalization. Researchers find that although boys and girls experience the same emotions, girls express their feelings more freely and more often.[1]

When we polled girls about words they most regret saying to their parents, the hands-down winner was "I hate you!"—a perfect example of emotion moving from brain to tongue the way kids go down a water slide. If your daughter is out there on an emotional edge from time to time, exaggerating and overreacting, she's sharing that space with lots of other girls her age.

That's because a girl of 7 or 10, and even 14, doesn't do much abstract thinking yet. Instead, she generally *feels* what she thinks. Let's say your daughter wants to play basketball on a team. When she wonders about this or imagines it, she is not analyzing what playing requires. She is feeling the thrill and excitement of playing with friends, dribbling the ball, and shooting in front of a crowd. Your daughter's emotions move in big zigs and zags. If she thinks about something pleasurable, her feelings soar upward. If she thinks about a difficult social studies test or missing her friends over summer break, her emotional state falls. Three years ago at a

---

1. Ann Kring, "Sex Differences in Emotion: Expression, Experience, and Physiology," *Journal of Personality and Social Psychology* 74, no. 3 (March 1998): 686–703. In this study, college students watched movie clips while their facial expressions and physical responses were videotaped and monitored by electrodes. Men and women registered the same physical reactions, but the females expressed themselves more freely in facial expression and verbal reports after the show.

neighborhood picnic, one of my daughters ran across the yard to me and nearly swooned at my feet. "I've met someone!" she cooed. "There's no one like him in the world!" I asked her about that incident recently. She doesn't remember the first thing about it. That was, I think, a minor zig.

Your daughter is working on building emotional firewalls, barriers between her thoughts and her feelings, so that her emotions won't be continually off the scale one way or the other.[2] This takes time and experience (the first 20 years of her life, more or less), and her learning curve is seldom going to be a smooth, upward-rising path. An 8-year-old girl, for example, may appear to deal with her emotions more successfully than her big sister who is 12—but that's because she's not coping with the same level of emotion. By age 12, girls are dealing with hormonal changes, increased social and academic pressures, and a broader emotional range. If it seems to you that your daughter is less emotionally mature than she used to be, that's understandable. It may look that way because as she begins to feel things more intensely, taming her emotions is harder than it used to be.

On top of that, every girl has her own emotional style. One of my daughters, Sara, is fairly circumspect. When she feels an emotion, she tends to hold it inside and look at it a bit before she acts on it. When her sister, Jean, feels an emotion, the whole family knows about it instantly. As I watch both my daughters learn to manage their strong feelings, I continue to learn how each girl needs a slightly different style of parenting. I let my own emotions range a

2. Daniel Goleman, *Emotional Intelligence: Why It Can Matter More than IQ* (New York: Bantam Books, 1996). In fact, much of your daughter's success and happiness in life will depend on learning to handle herself when her emotions are strong. The ability to recognize and manage her feelings is called "emotional intelligence," a set of skills first identified and explored by Goleman.

little more freely with Sara, because she usually doesn't overreact. But if she holds emotion inside too long, it wears her out and frays her self-esteem, so I keep a protective eye on her emotional well-being.

Meanwhile, Jean tends to express herself quickly and sometimes says things she regrets. I dampen my emotional responses a bit when dealing with her so that I won't add fuel to already burning fires. In other words, I tune my emotional antenna a little differently depending on which daughter I'm dealing with and the emotional state she's in. You do the same at your house. That's because, to an amazing degree, our brains and our daughters' brains are actually on the same wavelength.

When Two Brains Collide

Human brains are divided into three basic areas—the brain stem, the limbic system, and the cortex. The *brain stem* is the most primal part of the brain. It tells the heart to beat, the lungs to breathe, and the other organs to function. Wrapped around the brain stem is the *limbic system*. This is the emotional part of the brain. Fight-or-flight reactions originate here, as do affection, bonding, and sadness. Finally, there's the most recent evolutionary addition, the *cortex*. As the logical part of the brain, the cortex reasons things through and checks things out, trying to make sure the emotional limbic region isn't reacting too quickly or too extremely. When the limbic region yells "FIRE!" the cortex says, "Are you sure? Do you see flame? It might just be some smoke." Guess which part of your daughter's brain is still under development?

When a girl feels threatened, the limbic part of her brain goes into high gear. For example, when she's dealing with parental censure or limits, she feels a threat to her fragile, developing sense of self. That's just as dangerous to her limbic brain as a physical threat. So, if you say, "No, I don't think you're ready to audition for the next level dance class," and your daughter goes ballistic, it's because her inexperienced limbic system is in there screaming, "They think I'm no good!" This is when your daughter may say, "You hate me! I hate you, too, and I wish I'd never been born!" That's a limbic system in hyperdrive.

Here's the hard part. Your daughter's feelings are contagious, especially to you. Her brain's over-the-top limbic region actually has the power to excite your limbic system. This is a phenomenon called *limbic resonance,* and it means that the limbic brains of two mammals exchange signals—silent reverberations that communicate how each of us is feeling to the other. At some level, you and I pick up our daughters' emotions. As one mom told me, "My daughter whines exactly on my frequency."

There's a lot of truth in that. The limbic system is a sensing organ. Just as the eyes give us visual information, the limbic system gives us readings on our own and others' emotional states. If you feel angry or afraid, your daughter senses those feelings, even if you don't act on them or say anything about them. Whether she's euphoric or upset, you tune into her vibes, too—you can't help it.[3]

We're already linked to our daughters biologically, living in the same space, often sharing the same genes, and sending each other pheromonal signals night and day. On top of all our biological connections, the emotional parts of our brains continually trawl the family waters, asking, "So, how are we all feeling today?" This helps explain why hurtful exchanges can ignite before we know what

3. Maurice Elias, Steven Tobias, and Brian Friedlander, *Raising Emotionally Intelligent Teenagers* (New York: Harmony Books, 2000). A useful analysis of limbic resonance and how it affects the way we parent.

happened. It's also why exchanges with our daughters so seldom involve isolated zingers but turn into exchanges with lots of back-and-forth. We're already tuned to each other's channels, poised to reflect the feelings we find there. If you and I are broadcasting empathy and love, our daughters are likely to pick up those vibes, boost the signal, and send them back to us. The same goes for anger and frustration.

Piloting the Plane

So, when things are intense, who's going to put out the verbal fires? (Hint: Who has the mature cortex?) And who has to model emotional intelligence so that our daughters can learn to handle *their* emotions? You've got it. You and I are piloting the plane. It's not fair, but that's the deal. As parents, you and I can talk about our feelings; indeed, as role models, we should. But our daughters have dibs on overreacting—on screaming, acting out, attacking, name-calling, nasty comments, and all the rest.

No matter what my daughter's emotional state, no matter how upset I feel in response, my best course is not to overreact verbally. One mother who mastered the skill of giving herself time to think shared this example:

> Anna used to tell me that she hated me. That was so hurt-ful. But I finally figured out that if I would just go straight to my room, things would get better. That way I wouldn't react in front of her. In my room I could cry or scream or read to calm myself down.
>
> —Janet, mother of a 14-year-old girl

Adolescent girls are fearful people anyway. Down deep, they're afraid they can't handle the world. If you and I overreact, our daughters know we're afraid for them. Then they figure they *really* can't handle it. They rely on us for stability.

Keeping Your Cool

In the course of researching this book, I talked to many parents who told me their stories and offered wonderful advice. Many of them had overreacted in the past but then had figured out ways of minimizing their reactions when similar situations came up again. Parenting is like that: we learn on the job. Here are some of these parents' touchstones for staying calm when things are heating up between themselves and their daughters:

> *I try to say, "You could be right." That gives my daughter a second to cool down, and it makes me remember that she probably has a point I just don't understand yet.*
> *—Becky, mother of two girls, 14 and 16*

> *I try to step back in my head and ask, "What would an observer see now?" That helps me calm down.*
> *—Rick, father of an 11-year-old girl*

> *I tell myself, "You don't have to get in the last word."*
> *—Janice, mother of daughters ages 11 and 13*

> *I try to throw a wet blanket over my feelings and breathe deeply. I ask myself, "Is this something that I really have to react to?"*
> *—Trish, mother of a 14-year-old girl*

I try to focus on who's feeling what rather than on the content of the conversation.

—Neil, father of a 13-year-old girl

I tell my daughters, "If you want an answer now, the answer is no. If you can wait and let me think, the answer may be different."

—Deidra, mother of two daughters, 15 and 17

Notice how many of these parents use specific phrases or questions to help them get perspective? Any time we ask a question or repeat a calming mantra, we remind ourselves to stop and *think*, and that puts the calming cortex into gear. Thus, questions act like speed bumps on the highway to verbal collisions. Questions also signal curiosity about what our daughters are feeling and thinking, and curiosity about people means that we're connected to and concerned about them. Asking questions is a powerful internal signal for us, and those same questions serve as signals to our daughters, too. They let girls know we care.

Turning the Talk Around

Use the questions below when emotions start to spike between you and your daughter; they can help you move the conversation in a more positive direction.

Is this something to react to?

How can I bring some calmness to what is happening?

What can I do or say that will show her I'm listening?

What is she feeling? What can I say that will validate her feelings (and won't make things worse)?

What can I say that will express my own feelings (and won't make things worse)?

"I WAS JUST TEASING!"

Dad: *Those sure are ugly shoes you bought.*

Girl: *No, they're not.*

Dad: *Are you sure? I don't know when I've seen shoes that ugly.*

Girl: *They're not ugly. And it would hurt if someone kicked you with them, too!*

Dad: *Really? Do ugly shoes hurt worse when you get kicked with them?*

Girl: *Dad, quit it!*

Dad: *Calm down. I was just teasing!*

What Just Happened?

Teasing is a tricky subject. Some amount of teasing happens in most families, and gentle banter between parents and girls can feel quite affectionate. But many girls wrote about being hurt by parental teasing. Adults understand that affection often underlies teasing, but much of the time children experience teasing as hurtful. The very dynamic of teasing—saying that something about a person is inadequate or that there's something she doesn't know—emphasizes the power difference between two people.

> *My dad always joked and made fun of me. Sometimes it really got to me. I told him how I felt, and he apologized. Now there is a no-making-fun policy in my house.*
> —*Michelle, age 10*

This girl's story reminds us that dads usually tease daughters more than moms do. Boys use teasing as a way of showing girls they're interested in them. Girls with brothers tend to learn to take teasing in stride because that's one way their brothers know how to relate to them. Dads were boys once, and so they still tend to tease girls as an indirect way of showing their affection.

The *subject* of our teasing matters, too. Teasing a girl about anything she feels vulnerable about is not funny to her. For example, you'd never want to tease a girl about liking a boy she actually likes. By the same token, if she is shorter than her classmates, overweight, or underdeveloped, teasing her about her body size would be cruel. In contrast, a girl who once mistook one uncle for another (because people look alike on that side of the family) and was mildly embarrassed might find "No, that's Uncle Bob" to be funny later on. There's a difference between laughing *with* our daughters and laughing *at* them—a difference they feel keenly.

What If You Said . . .

W ords showing that you understand she feels hurt can help mend the harm that teasing causes.

I love you so much, and sometimes I tease you because I want to have fun with you. But I can see it really isn't fun for you. What can we do or talk about together instead?

I'm used to teasing people I like, but I can see it hurts your feelings.

My brothers and sisters teased each other a lot when I was growing up. And because I grew up being used to it, I sort of expected you to be able to deal with it, too. I do respect your wishes for me not to do this. I'm sorry.

When I tease you, I don't mean to hurt your feelings, but I guess I do. I'll try to remember how much it upsets you.

"DON'T SWEAR AT ME!"

Dad: *You forgot to take the garbage to the curb again. You forgot it last week, too. Now it's all piled up. I don't want to come in off the road and find this kind of mess!*

Girl: *It's hard to remember trash day. I've got so much other stuff to keep up with.*

Dad: *We ALL have plenty to keep up with. This is the one thing I ask you to remember. Damn it! If you'd get off the computer long enough to think straight, maybe you'd do your chores for a change.*

Girl: *Hell, Dad, I do my best!*

What Just Happened?

When we swear at our daughters, we are, for a moment, disregarding the value of the relationship and stepping outside our role as parent and guide. Swearing *around* our daughters but not at them is also a problem, although some of us consider it a milder one. We parents have rights to our strong feelings, just as our daughters do. Sometimes "Damn it!" gets closer to what I'm feeling than "I'm really upset about this." That said, even this kind of swearing can be a problem, because curses are such hard words, and the girls we love hear plenty of hard words in the world outside our homes. In the best of worlds, we provide our daughters a safe haven at home, a respite from words that demean or hurt.

Swearing around our daughters sends the message that we have just included them in our adult world. As a result, they feel invited and entitled to swear back—and given the chance, they generally do. When that happens, we're faced with a decision about

how to react and are left with darn little to say, because we have
abandoned the high ground by swearing in the first place.

What If You Said . . .

If you've cursed and wish that you hadn't, explain your regret and
clarify how you'd like to handle the situation in the future.

*I'm so sorry I used that kind of language with you. When you don't
do what I have expected you to do, I get angrier than I should.
And cursing only makes both of us feel worse.*

*Look, let's not talk to each other this way. I feel awful when I hear
you curse, and I'll bet you feel upset when I do. I'll keep my cool
next time, and maybe that will help you do the same.*

*Swearing and cursing come so easily sometimes. I'm going to
remember how important it is to try to stay in control, because
that is what you expect of me—just like I expect you to do your
chores.*

"YOU'RE SO SELFISH!"

Girl: *I can't get dressed. I told you I needed new jeans, but you didn't do anything about it, and now I don't have anything to wear.*

Mom: *You have plenty of clothes, honey. Just wear something else.*

Girl: *My other pants are all too small. I told you that before. Are you deaf or something?*

Mom: *Don't talk to me like that! Why is it you never appreciate all I do for you? You're so selfish!*

What Just Happened?

We spend years teaching our daughters to trust us—answering their calls from the crib, running furiously when they are close to disaster, singing their praises when they succeed, supporting them all along the way with words of encouragement. When this trust that develops during infancy is reaffirmed again and again as our daughters grow, it helps them feel strong and sure of themselves. But in one single moment, we can destroy that scaffold of trust with labeling and derision.

When frustrations build between parents and daughters, insults and labels often follow. The girls we surveyed reported being called *selfish, stupid, lazy, monster, dummy, nerd,* and, most frequently, *spoiled* by their parents. They also admitted flinging similar labels back.

Whether they admit it or not, girls take us at our word. Until your daughter enters adolescence, she generally is going to accept what you say as true. Even when she's 14 years old, you are still her bedrock, and your words are the primary truth she knows. For good or ill, she hears you. Deep down, our daughters believe what we tell them about themselves.

*Once my mom called me stupid. I felt hurt inside because
how am I supposed to talk to her now if other people call
me stupid?*

—Tina, age 9

Once Tina's mom has said Tina is stupid, this nine-year-old is
at a complete loss. As she points out, she has no one else to turn to,
no defender left to tell her that this isn't true.

The labels we give girls are powerful—even predictive.
If the words a girl hears from us are critical and rejecting, she is
primed to grow up thinking that she is not good enough and that
she doesn't deserve love.

What If You Said . . .

If you've said something insulting to your daughter, correct it
immediately and often. Calm down and address her behavior,
not her character.

*I shouldn't have said that. It isn't true. When you speak to me with
disrespect, it's easy for me to get frustrated.*

*You and I are having a hard day today, but I don't believe you're
selfish. Not for a minute. I love you so much that my heart
hurts when we're at odds like this. But I do need you to speak
to me with respect.*

*Wow, it's amazing how quickly insults can get started between us.
I'm going to try not to do that again. I didn't mean what I said.*

"YOU ONLY ADOPTED ME!"

Girl: *Is it okay if I go with Martina and her mother to the mall?*

Mom: *You know the deal was that you couldn't go anywhere until you folded your laundry and cleared the dishes. You had all day, and I don't want your laundry all over the sofa any longer.*

Girl: *But Mom, we've been planning this all week. You knew.*

Mom: *Yes, and you knew that the laundry and dishes would be your responsibility. You have bargained and bargained with me, but I don't think that you can leave these things another minute.*

Girl: *So punish me again! You like doing that, especially when my best friends invite me somewhere. My real mom would understand, but you're not even related to me. You only adopted me!*

Mom: *Well, your real mom's not here! I'm the one you're stuck with!*

What Just Happened?

No matter how happy a girl is with her adoptive parents, there are two relationships in her life that are broken—those with her biological mom and dad. Sometimes a girl fears her birth parents gave her up because she was flawed or unlovable, and sometimes that insecurity surfaces with a vengeance, causing an adopted daughter to lash out.

Some adoptive daughters get into the habit of blaming nearly every unhappiness on their adoptive parents. Then they feel guilty for not loving us enough, even though we adopted them. At the same time, we may feel guilty—ironically—because we aren't their birth parents and wish we could be. Don't be surprised if your daughter's reminder that you aren't her birth parent prompts you to grieve (again) the biological children you couldn't or didn't have.

All of these feelings are complex and messy.

If your daughter uses her adoption against you, remember that nearly every adopted daughter does this at some point. It's developmental more than it is personal. (Even girls who live with their birth moms yell, "I wish you weren't my mom!") Understanding that adopted daughters tend to feel a chronic sense of loss is a great beginning. That alone will help you respect, and not sugarcoat or discount, her feelings when they come up. On the other hand, you have to let her know that you deserve her respect and are not willing to carry guilt for her loss.

When your relationship gets stormy, remember to give yourself credit for all the things you've done well for your daughter, find support if you need it, and give your daughter time. As a young adult, she'll be more likely to appreciate your love and care.

What If You Said . . .

If your daughter uses her adoption against you, she is expressing loss and testing you, hoping you'll affirm your connection to her.

I'm sorry I said that. It must hurt not to have your birth mom around. That's one reason I give you all the love I do—because we all need a mom. But right now we need to talk about chores. I need you to do your work before you go to the mall.

You often bring up your birth mother when we disagree. I know you miss knowing her, and I'm sorry. That doesn't distract me from the fact that your chores have to get done. Birth moms and adoptive moms expect their daughters to be responsible.

I'm sorry I said you were stuck with me. I'd never change that. But I'm trying to be the kind of mom who teaches you responsibility. I feel firm about this—you have to do your chores.

"WHAT DID YOU JUST CALL ME?"

Girl: *You're late again to pick me up. I <u>hate</u> standing here waiting for you. Don't you even care that I'm out here all alone?*

Mom: *Don't do this today, Pam. Let's not get started down this road again. I've had a long day.*

Girl: *Fine. So I just have to be quiet and wait late and put up with you never being on time. Like I'm some loser, too.*

Mom: *That's <u>enough</u>. You're just getting to be a little witch, aren't you?*

Girl: *(beneath her breath) Bitch!*

What Just Happened?

Not long ago I talked with a group of sixth-grade girls. They dutifully answered my questions about parents and words, but I wasn't getting much participation, so I decided to try a show of hands. "Let's vote," I said. "Is yelling ever okay? Raise your hand if you think it is." The vote was split, with sensible reasons offered on both sides. "How about name-calling?" I asked. This time, there was no hesitation. "Never" and "No" resounded before we even voted, and heads were shaking "no" on every side. The vote was unanimous. "Why?" I asked. "It hurts too bad," one girl answered. "And you have to sort of believe them."

Name-calling may be the most destructive verbal violation of a relationship, especially when we're dealing with children. Girls do believe us, and even if they don't believe everything we say, they trust that our judgment is accurate. So when we call our daughters *tramps* or *jerks* or any other ill-chosen slam, those words sink in deep and stay inside a very long time. **Girls don't forget the names we call them.**

Any time words are very harsh or physical violence is a possibility, your best option is to walk away. The mom in this scenario may need to stop the car, get out and walk around, or drop her daughter at home and go out for a cup of coffee—anything that ends the sparring immediately, soothes the senses, and gives both people a chance to cool down.

Name-calling is almost always an indication of serious problems in the relationship, a sign that something is broken. If you and your daughter call each other names, don't hesitate to seek help. Talk with a therapist, your minister, or a trusted friend.

What If You Said . . .

If either you or your daughter has fallen into a pattern of name-calling, try these words to slow down the escalation of emotion.

This is hurting us both. I apologize. Can we calm down and talk?

I should never call you names. We need to work this out, but right now I have to go away and cool down.

I want our relationship to be better than it is. I am going to work on respecting you more. You deserve my respect. And I hope you'll try to respect me more as well.

I feel really sad that we do this to each other. We're having so much trouble getting along that I want to find somebody who can hear us out and help us solve our problems.

You are so important to me. Let's call (a counselor, our minister, a trusted friend) and talk with (him/her) about what's going on. We need to figure out some ways not to hurt each other.

"ALL YOU DO IS CRITICIZE"

Girl: *(to her sister) Well, Dannie is okay sometimes, but mostly she is too bossy.*

Sister: *The worst. And her brother is weird—have you noticed? (laughing) He never brushes his teeth!*

Girl: *How could I miss it? He is so gross!*

Mom: *Hey, you two, think about what you're saying. Dannie would be really hurt if she could hear this conversation.*

Girl: *But she can't hear us, and what we're saying is true. Dannie thinks she is so cool, but she is weird. So is her whole family.*

Mom: *Stop it right now! All you do is criticize. Why can't you ever say anything positive about anybody?*

What Just Happened?

Sometimes, especially when social competition at school is fierce, a girl can get stuck in a habitual put-down mode. This unpleasant behavior is usually based in an insecurity that is, to some degree, developmental. In order to define herself, a girl may comment long and loud about what she doesn't like about others—making it clear, she hopes, that she is not like (and, on the contrary, superior to) the people she is criticizing.

At other times, a girl in early adolescence bad-mouths others as a first-strike tactic. She expects (sometimes rightly so) that other girls will talk negatively about her, so she throws a defensive verbal punch by saying negative things first.

Finally, talking about others helps girls bond with other girls. Talking about someone who is not there is a way of establishing rapport with the person who is there.

Even if you understand all the possible motivations behind a girl's "dissing" of friends and family, that doesn't mean you ought to condone or ignore it. We all expect a higher standard of behavior from our daughters. The problem is figuring out how to say that in a way that helps a girl become thoughtful instead of reactionary.

What If You Said . . .

If your daughter seems compelled to put others down, look for words that come from a loving place rather than a critical one. Otherwise, you can end up criticizing her criticism—which may compel her to hold her ground.

I notice that I start to feel tense when I hear you criticize other people. Can you understand how your negative comments make other people feel negative, too? Let's talk about something else.

We're in very different places on this. I feel hurt for Dannie when I hear you talk about her unkindly.

When you are so negative about others, I worry that you're losing your sense of compassion. And that's something I really value about you—your loving heart.

Does it feel satisfying to you to criticize Dannie and her brother? Could you explain why?

This may be hard for you to imagine today, but you'll look back in a year or two and recognize what you're doing now as cruel, even if it doesn't feel that way to you right now.

I know it can be fun to talk about other people. I've done it, too. But I hope you won't make it a habit. It diminishes us when we speak badly of others. I know you're sensitive and compassionate, and I don't think that talk is typical of you.

"I HATE YOU! I WISH YOU WEREN'T MY DAD!"

Girl: *... But why don't you have the money for me to go to an extra week of equestrian camp? You have money for lots of other things.*

Dad: *We had a budget for your summer camps, remember? An extra week at that camp wasn't one of the choices you made.*

Girl: *Kellie is going for the whole summer! I've got to be there, too!*

Dad: *It isn't going to work this year.*

Girl: *I hate you! I mean it. I wish you weren't my dad!*

What Just Happened?

This book is full of subjects that can cause friction between daughters and parents. But a disagreement about *any* of those subjects—food or rules or privacy or boys—can be the precursor to the kinds of words you see on this page. When any conflict escalates and we feel at a loss as to how to proceed, we have a tendency to turn on each other by attacking our connections to each other. The toughest words to hear your daughter say are probably "I hate you." But other statements come from the same painful place in her heart, including "I wish I'd never been born," "I wish you were dead," and "You're the worst mom/dad in the world."

When the parent-daughter relationship is attacked, our limbic systems—and our hearts—sense a threat like no other. It's bad enough for you and me, but it feels even more threatening for our less-mature daughters. Even when a girl herself makes the attack, she cannot keep from fearing the power of her own words—that they might come true. If your daughter attacks the relationship, consider it a sign that she has been hurt and is trying to hurt you in return—not that she means her words literally.

*Sometimes when I'm steamed about something and I don't
feel my parents understand, I will randomly say things I
don't even mean, like "You don't even love me" or "I wish I
wasn't your daughter."*

—Roz, age 13

This girl's choice of the word "randomly" is a clue. The content
of what she says isn't what counts most to her at times like this.
What counts is that she gets to assert her hurt.

What If You Said . . .

If your daughter attacks her relationship with you, walk away if
you need to. Do something to soothe yourself (after all, you have
to take good care of yourself in order to do this hard job of parenting!). Focus on the feelings behind your daughter's words, and try:

I can hear how upset you are. I'm listening.

*I know it's hard to be in this family sometimes. It's not a perfect
family, but we all do the best we can.*

*Those are very strong words. They have a lot of power. I hope that
later you'll apologize for saying them.*

*I feel really sad when you say that. Let's try not to talk to each other
that way if we can help it.*

*I think we should end this conversation for now, because it's so
hard for both of us to get a hold on our emotions. Let's take a
break or a walk and come back and try again.*

CHAPTER

Food Fights and Body Size
How can we nourish our daughters without being overly controlling? How can we express concern about a girl's body size with words that don't make matters worse?

---

*One time when I was getting some cookies after dinner,
my dad said that I was getting "piggy." I got really mad.
I told him I wasn't going to talk to him again, but he
came by my room and said he was sorry. I guess parents
can make mistakes . . .*

—Bette, age 13

*When my daughter was younger, she would come home
from having had dinner at one of her friends' houses and
sit down at our table and begin eating what was left. This
would make me very anxious, and eventually I'd say
something like, "Didn't you eat at Sarah's house?" or
"Are you still hungry?" Of course she saw straight through
me, and now I know that all these questions were hurtful,
even though my intent was to make her stop and think
before eating food she didn't need and maybe even didn't
want. I was confusing my own feelings with her needs
and desires, and I was alienating her in the process.*

—Mary, the mother of two daughters

Nothing connects us to our daughters more fundamentally than food. From the day they are born, we feed their bodies. Year after year, we shop for them, cook for them, and sit down with them to eat. Meanwhile, they go through various stages, sometimes being picky eaters and at other times eating everything in the kitchen.

As they get older, our daughters start to figure out what foods suit them best, in what proportions and at what hours of the day. Meanwhile, we're trying to get them to eat the traditional "balanced three." No wonder we have misunderstandings—and harsh words.

Food has deeper meanings, too. All of us, girls and parents alike, have an emotional "hunger" for each other. A friend of mine describes the wistfulness she feels when her children are away at summer camp as "L.O.K."—lack of kids. "They come home," my friend says, "and I fill myself up with them again."

We are supposed to hunger for the warmth and joy we know is possible within the parent-daughter bond. We are meant to miss each other when we're apart or at odds. So sometimes the food we use to feed our daughters' bodies becomes a symbol for feeding emotional hunger, too—theirs and our own. Because food plays such a powerful role in our lives, it can be a peace treaty, a celebration, or even an apology. An offering of food can say "I love you" or "Let's make up."

One night Susan and I fought, and I called her "selfish"
and instantly regretted it. The next morning I got up, tip-
toed downstairs, and made a favorite omelet for her. When
she saw that, she smiled and said, "Thank you, Mommy."
Then we began to talk about what went wrong the night
before.

—*Lynn, mother of a 14-year-old girl*

But food can be used to manipulate as well. A meal on the table
can signal "I control you; eat this" to a girl who needs more input
into what she eats and when. Her refusal to eat can be a way of
telling a parent, "I don't like what you like. I'm not you. I'm me."
Where food is concerned, our fear is usually expressed as control.
If you and your daughter are in conflict because you're trying to
control her eating, ask, "What am I afraid of?" This can help you
gain perspective and let go a little.

The Pressures on Girls

Then there's body size. This issue comes into play every time we
talk to girls about food. It's hard for us to imagine how much
pressure our daughters feel to be a prescribed size and shape.
Even in preschool, they know that being pudgy is somehow wrong
or bad. In elementary school, overweight girls are almost certain to
be teased or harassed.

Researchers find that by age seven, a girl's attitude about her
body shape has formed, and as many as half of today's eight- and
nine-year-old girls are dissatisfied with their size and long to be
thinner. Meanwhile, fast food and snack machines are everywhere
our daughters go, so it's not always easy for them to make good

choices. On top of that, a girl's body repeatedly goes through cycles of filling out and then shooting up throughout childhood and adolescence. One day a girl finds that her clothes are all too tight; two months later she's thin again but now everything is too short. Girls often worry during these filling-out phases. Food—what they eat, how much, and how they feel about it afterward—triggers anxiety.

Given all that pressure, it's hard for us to talk to girls about food, diets, and the size of their bodies, and it's hard for girls to *hear* us, too.

> *Once when I picked out a shirt I liked, my mom said, "Oh, honey, that is not going to fit you. You need a bigger size." It hurt my feelings!*
>
> *—Nancy, age 11*

Everything we say to girls about body size—even if it's just a reference to perfectly normal growth—can be laced with unintended hurt. And even the best-intentioned conversations can go wrong:

> *My mama has always wanted me to get outside and play sports, but I'd rather write in my journal, bake treats, or make crafts. Once she tried to explain to me that I was overweight and needed some exercise. I told her no, and then things got out of hand. She ended up calling me a lazy pig! I ran up to my room and lay on the bed and cried, because kids had made fun of me for being fat, but never my own mother.*
>
> *—Beverly, age 11*

Luckily, this story has a happy ending. After Beverly's mother lost control, she and her daughter talked again:

> *My mom told me that what she'd said wasn't true. She said she just cared about me, and exercising could make me healthier. We made a deal that once a day I'd go downstairs and dance with her, because I love to dance, and that is a form of exercise. Now we have everything worked out, plus I am getting thinner and I feel better!*
>
> *—Beverly, age 11*

Her Body, Her Identity

Ask a school-age girl to describe herself, and her first statements will be body-based and concrete: "I have brown eyes and black hair" or "I'm tall and I have brown hair." A girl's body simply *is* her baseline self, her primary identity. And we parents shape her sense of self, too. We tell our daughters who they are, and, whether they admit it or not, they believe us. When we cherish and respect our daughters' bodies, our girls feel good about who they are inside and out. But if we say dismissive or offensive things about their bodies, we shake our daughters' confidence to the core.

> *One time my mother told me that I'd better be careful about what I ate, because I was getting fat! That really hurt my feelings, because I often get teased at school about my size. But then to hear it from my mom was just worse, worse, worse.*
>
> *—Gwen, age 9*

This puts us in a bind when we talk to our daughters about eating. On the one hand, we want to guide them toward healthy food choices. On the other hand, we can hurt girls more deeply than anybody else can. In the process of walking this fine line, we can easily say too little, too much, or the wrong thing entirely. In this chapter, we'll explore words we can use to ally with our daughters when they struggle with food and body size. We'll talk about letting go when it's time, as well as about trusting our daughters' growing bodies and healthy hungers.

So read on. It's good for you, like broccoli.

Words About Weight

When you talk with your daughter about her body size, keep these ideas in mind:

Focus on growth and health, not on weight. Be sure to talk about how various stages of growth cause girls to change shape—that she's supposed to get wider hips and a bigger, stronger body as she goes through puberty.

Do not ask how much she weighs or ask her to weigh herself. Do stress that you want her to be healthy and be able to run fast and jump high.

Compliment the whole girl. As the days go by, monitor your comments about your daughter. How often do you comment on her appearance as opposed to her character or her ability? Be sure to let her know that you "see" her whole self—her spirit and her intellect—not just her body. Frequent use of "You're a great kid" actually goes a lot further toward helping your daughter maintain a healthy weight than does "How much do you weigh now?"

"YUCK! THIS FOOD IS GROSS"

Girl: *What do we have for dinner?*

Mom: *Baked chicken, green beans, potatoes.*

Girl: *Yuck! I hate chicken and green beans. I've told you a million times! Why do you always cook such gross food?*

Mom: *This is what I made for you. It's so upsetting when you don't eat what I cook! Why are you so ungrateful?*

What Just Happened?

We need our school-age daughters to eat the food we make—for convenience's sake and for their good health. But sometimes we also want them to eat because the food we give them represents our love for them, and this can get us into trouble. If I cook green beans and put them on the dinner table, they *do* represent my care and nurturance for my family. Yet, green beans are just green beans. If my daughter doesn't eat them, it has nothing, really, to do with her feelings for me, just for or against green beans. She *does,* however, need to be polite with me about her green bean–related feelings.

Why might your daughter criticize a meal? First of all, she arrives at mealtime with a set of issues all her own. If she refuses your pot roast, she may simply have had a terrible day at school and need to let off steam. She may have realized she doesn't like pot roast anymore. Or she may have had a hefty serving of protein at lunch so that her body isn't hungry for meat again. The problem is that she probably isn't mature enough to verbalize those notions. Instead, she insults the food, or you. At the same time that you are obligated—and *want*—to feed her, you also have to give her room to figure out what she likes and doesn't like. This can be difficult.

One thing is certain—if you buy into the food-equals-love equation, you are virtually *set up* to be jerked around emotionally just because your daughter doesn't eat her pot roast. In cases like this, offering alternative foods does not mean you're giving in. It just means you're taking a healthy step back from the food-equals-love assumption. It's a way of saying, "It's my responsibility to feed you, but I know your body is your own." (That said, be careful not to let yourself become a short-order cook preparing numerous menus.)

You can tell your daughter that her rude tone is not acceptable and inform her about her options for dinner. Then consider changing the subject; she'll know you heard the slight and didn't like it, but you won't force a showdown. In the course of conversation, she is likely to find an opportunity to catch your eye and let you know she's sorry.

What If You Said . . .

If your daughter rejects what you fix, remember that food is one area where girls routinely assert individuality. Talk with her about helping to choose and fix some simple alternatives herself.

I understand you don't like chicken and green beans, but I wish you'd find a more respectful way of saying so. Try that again.

Since everybody else in the family does like this food, we're bound to have it once in a while. Why don't you fix yourself a sandwich and eat that at dinner instead? I'll help you if you need me to.

I think you can tell me that in a less hurtful way. I remember when you used to like chicken. Are your tastes changing?

Let's see. If you don't have the chicken and beans, you won't be getting protein or vegetables. So let's look in the fridge and see if there's anything you can substitute.

"YOU CAN'T MAKE ME!"

Dad: *Eat your broccoli, please.*

Girl: *No. I don't want to.*

Dad: *But it's good for you. It makes you grow strong.*

Girl: *Ugh—no way! You can't make me!*

Dad: *No, but I can take away TV. And I will if you don't eat that broccoli.*

What Just Happened?

By their very nature, food choices are personal and individual. Food that makes you feel full and energized might leave your daughter feeling empty, and vice versa. Food that tastes good to her may not taste good to you. This is important to remember when our daughters make what appear to be poor choices, or choices that are inconvenient for the family schedule or routine.

Individual tastes and nutritional needs aren't the only factors at work here. When a girl wants to remind us that she is an individual, the dinner table is usually one of the first places her message is borne out. After all, eating what someone else gives you to eat— especially if you don't have a hand in planning the menu—feels submissive to a kid who is actively trying to figure out how to be her own person and let the world know she is. Consider this girl:

> *I was having dinner, and my food was at the spot that I usually sit at, but I was sitting somewhere else. When my mom said, "Your food's getting cold," I said, "I want it over here. Why else would I be sitting here?" Then she looked at me with this funny look and I felt really bad.*
>
> *—Nita, age 12*

If your daughter resists eating what's on the table, try stepping inside the circle of her feelings. Maybe she doesn't like this food. Maybe she feels confined or, like Nita, guilty. If possible, give your daughter alternative choices and trade-offs. Not only will you avoid hurtful conflict, but you'll also help her learn to regulate her own eating. Girls whose food choices are too closely regimented by their parents tend to grow up making poor food choices, but girls whose parents give them guidelines and choices usually become good self-regulators as teens and young adults.

What If You Said . . .

Use words like these to avoid turning your daughter's food choices into a power struggle between you:

Of course I don't want to make you eat the broccoli. That would feel terrible to both of us. Help me understand why it's something you don't want.

I can hear how mad you are. Help me understand why.

I need to know that you eat some vegetables every day. I feel like it's my job to help you eat right. Is there a vegetable you'd like to eat instead of the broccoli?

Look, it makes me feel good when you eat the food I make. But the bottom line is that I want to know you eat a variety of healthy foods daily. Did you have any veggies today? Any fruits?

We could compromise. You eat the broccoli tonight, and you can help me plan tomorrow night's menu so that you know we'll have something you like better.

"I'M A VEGETARIAN NOW"

Mom: *Have some chicken and pass it, please.*

Girl: *I don't want chicken. I'm not eating dead animals anymore.*

Mom: *What?*

Girl: *Do you know what they do to chickens? They pump them full of steroids and leave the lights on 24 hours a day. And their beaks are cut off so they won't peck each other to . . .*

Mom: *That's enough! You're ruining everybody's dinner.*

Girl: *So? The chicken's whole life was ruined.*

What Just Happened?

Lots of girls are drawn to vegetarianism, usually for highly ideal-istic reasons. This is completely normal and healthy behavior for a school-age or adolescent girl. During these years, she is *supposed* to experiment with her food choices and figure out what feels right for her body. She is also exploring right and wrong, fairness and justice. A compassionate girl can easily decide she shouldn't eat meat, processed foods, or dairy products. So, when she makes this kind of announcement, we have to remember that this is not about us, her parents. It is about herself, her developing character, and the person she is trying to figure out how to become.

If you're like me, it's hard to hear your daughter reject the food you're offering her. It's even harder if she condemns your own eating habits in the process. Being attacked at your own kitchen table for eating things your daughter suddenly will no longer touch can make you both angry and fearful. Any time a girl sets off on a course of eating that's different from before, we parents lose a little more control over an aspect of a girl's life that we used to control completely. That's new. It's also perfectly normal. In cases like these, our daughters are doing exactly what we want them to do—taking stands based on conscience and examining how their actions impact the world.

You and I have a choice when confronted by this kind of situation. We can try to maintain control, or we can let go just a little and help the girls we love explore new paths that may have meaning for them. For a younger girl, this may mean making sure she knows the cottage cheese and hard-boiled eggs you leave in the refrigerator are good substitutes for meat. For an older girl, it might mean teaching her to cook with tofu. In either case, you'll probably want to talk with a nutritionist, so that both you and your daughter can learn more about meeting her nutritional needs.

What If You Said . . .

Giving your daughter a chance to tell you about her desire to be a vegetarian—at the right time and place—can help her feel acknowledged and valued.

This is a sudden announcement, so I'm having trouble knowing what to say. If you'll spare us the grim details about the lives of chickens right now, I'll hear you out after dinner.

I can see you feel strongly about this. When did you start thinking about becoming a vegetarian?

It's clear you're moved by the suffering of animals—that's very compassionate. I admire that. I also think we each have the right to make our own decisions about what we choose to eat. Please be respectful of my decision, and I'll be respectful of yours.

Giving up meat is a big adjustment for your body. I guess I worry that you won't get the right nutrients or have enough energy. Can we talk about how you'll get enough protein?

"YOU'RE GETTING CHUBBY"

Mom: *Don't eat that last muffin. You've already had two.*

Girl: *But they're so good.*

Mom: *I know you like them, but I want you to stop eating so much, honey. You're getting chubby.*

Girl: *(lowers her head; silence)*

Mom: *I don't mean to hurt your feelings, but I'm getting worried about your weight.*

What Just Happened?

Body size is a sensitive issue, connected to so much shame in our culture that there is virtually no easy way to begin a discussion about it with our daughters. Not only does a girl bring her fears and insecurities to the discussion, but we parents bring our own fears, too. If a girl is truly overweight, we worry about her health, and, even if a girl is only a bit chubby, we worry that she'll be hurt by teasing, exclusion, or harassment.

At the base of all this anxiety is our love. We have profound, visceral connections to our daughters. To some degree, we can't keep from feeling what our daughters feel. If your daughter is ashamed of her weight, you intuit her distress. Perhaps you cringe when she eats an extra doughnut, and you hurt for her if she isn't fast enough to make the track team. We can't help it—our daughters' successes make us feel proud, and we feel sad for them when they fail. It may sound silly, but a few extra pounds around a girl's middle can make parents—mom and dad alike—ill at ease, even afraid. And fear often leads us to say things we regret later.

If you're a dad, your unease with your daughter's weight gain may express itself in teasing. Many of the girls who wrote to

American Girl mentioned that their dads called them nicknames like "chunky monkey" or "little piggy" as a way of getting the message across. Moms were more likely to express their fears directly. Both methods can cause unintentional hurt.

What If You Said . . .

If you need to talk with your daughter about weight, be aware of the sadness and shame she probably feels. Focus on her health and energy level rather than on her body size.

I'm worried you aren't getting enough exercise. Lots of kids don't these days. Let's think of some ways you can be more active.

I've noticed you seem to be changing in size. How are you feeling about that?

I know it's hard for girls to stay healthy these days with so much junk food everywhere you go and not many chances to exercise. All that makes me worry about you.

I have to admit, I've always been afraid of being fat. So I get scared if I think you might be gaining weight. Do you feel that way, too?

You're the greatest kid in the world. Period. That's what I see every time I look at you.

Being careful to make good food choices all of the time is so hard, I know! It is mainly a matter of balancing the calories you take in, which become energy, with those you use up exercising. How our bodies work is an interesting thing to learn more about. Maybe we could talk to a nutritionist to find out what your body needs at your age.

NOT IN FRONT OF HER FRIENDS

Girl: *(to her friend at a wedding reception) This thing is going on all day. I'm getting bored.*

Friend: *I know. The only thing to do is eat. Here comes your dad.*

Dad: *Hi, girls.*

Girl: *Hi, Dad. When are we going home?*

Dad: *Soon. Listen, that's enough food. You've been eating all day.*

Girl: *(face reddening and tears welling) I can't believe you said that, like I'm a pig or something. I haven't even been eating much!*

What Just Happened?

This dad has stumbled into hurtful territory. Simply by criticizing his daughter's eating habits, he has been unkind, and by doing this in public, in front of his daughter's friend, he compounds the betrayal. Whether our daughters are prepubescent eight-year-olds or girls in their teens, they depend on us to help them feel good about themselves. They desperately need us to affirm them—especially in public, where they feel most vulnerable.

You may not realize it, but school-age girls pretty much "keep watch" all the time, comparing themselves to others, assessing everybody's reactions to them, and scanning everybody's interactions with each other. The girl in the preceding scenario was probably thinking something that went like this: *What did Elizabeth think when I said that to her about the reception? . . . Does she think it's boring, too? . . . She is friends with Shelia. I wonder if they ever talk about me? . . . I'm not as thin as Shelia but maybe as thin as Elizabeth.*

Making all the urgent calculations that help a girl maintain her public face is challenging, even frightening. If her parent (the very foundation of a girl's identity and the person she should always be able to depend on to support her) criticizes her in public, the words have double bite.

All of us, girls and parents alike, are aware of how other people assess us when we're in public. That's why our fears can so easily ambush us then. This dad may not even have been aware that he was feeling uncomfortable with how much his daughter was eating until he started talking to her. He just wanted to make the food struggle go away for himself and for her. He wanted to end the discomfort he felt as he watched her eat. If you are feeling anxious about your daughter's body size or eating habits, do follow your instincts and tell her about your concerns. But find a time to do this privately, and try to be very aware of your own feelings, and own them, as you talk.

What If You Said . . .

If you've said something in public about your daughter's eating or her body size, do all you can to restore her dignity.

Of course you haven't been eating all day. I just know how easy it is for me to stand around talking and eat too much at these events, so I was worried you would, too. I said the wrong thing.

Gosh, I didn't mean anything by that. I am always on edge when an event like this goes on so long. You're the prettiest girl at this party. Wanna dance?

How could I say something so clumsy? I was just thinking that it's boring to stand around eating all day. How about if you and I get out of here and take a walk?

"DAD, DO YOU THINK I'M FAT?"

Girl: *Do you think I'm fat?*

Dad: *No.*

Girl: *Really?*

Dad: *Well, maybe you could stand to lose a <u>little</u> weight.*

Girl: *That's the worst thing you've ever said to me! (runs to her room crying)*

What Just Happened?

When girls wrote to American Girl about hurtful words related to food and body size, their dads' comments were cited again and again. If you're a dad, your words have extraordinary power in this arena. "On vacation, my dad told me I had to pay attention to my weight!" one girl wrote. "I cried a lot!" To her dad, this comment may have seemed like no big deal, simply a fact he mentioned. Not to his daughter. Whatever you say to your daughter about her body is something she'll soak in, believe, and react to strongly. Your daughter watches you to learn how men think and act. She listens to you to find out what men and boys are going to think about her. Words you don't even remember are likely to speak volumes to your daughter now and for years to come.

Yes, that's a terrible burden—but it's a gift as well. You have a unique ability to help your daughter grow up feeling good about herself. Be careful not to comment directly on your daughter's body shape or parts of her body, but do tell her often that she's growing up to be beautiful.

Also, many dads tend to be "fixers," offering solutions in an attempt to set things right. Sometimes dads suggest, "Just stop eating sweets," or "Take smaller servings," thinking that's all it will take—case closed. But girls often need more than that from you if you're a dad. Think of yourself as your daughter's ally in her struggle with food. If your daughter tells you how she feels about eating, being thin, or being heavy, be sure to listen closely. Try to echo back what she says about her feelings so she'll know that you heard her on this important issue. Finally, assure her that she is absolutely lovely, no matter what her size or shape, and that you know for sure this won't be a problem for her forever.

What If You Said . . .

If your daughter puts you on the spot with a question about her weight, respond with acceptance and try to get at why she might be concerned.

I've noticed you're changing size, but I definitely don't think you're fat. I like how you look.

Tell me more about what you're thinking. Maybe I can help.

You are a beautiful girl, and don't ever believe anybody who tells you otherwise.

The first time I saw you when you were a baby, I thought, "Wow, she's beautiful." And you've only gotten prettier and prettier.

Body image today has become so distorted, with girls wanting to look like models. We can get brainwashed to think that only those images are beautiful, when people come in lots of different sizes and shapes. You're beautiful, kiddo. Don't ever forget it.

"YOU'RE FAT, MOM"

Mom: *Those jeans look great on you. Let's buy them and go home.*

Girl: *Okay. I'm hurrying.*

Mom: *(studying herself in the mirror) I didn't realize these pants were so tight. I must have gained weight.*

Girl: *I know. You're getting fat, Mom. Oops! Just kidding! Just kidding!*

What Just Happened?

If you are uncomfortable with your own body shape, your daughter knows it. Our daughters always recognize our vulnerabilities. If your daughter is likely to attack your body size, you'll probably get some warnings when she's eight or nine years old. That's when she's likely to make little jokes about your size or shape. At that stage, she'll probably apologize or say, "Just teasing." Just testing is more like it, gauging your level of sensitivity.

In fact, your feelings about your body are a matter of great concern to your daughter. If you seem unhappy with your body or feel your body is out of control, your daughter feels pressure and discomfort, too. Because she is so closely connected to you, she's bound to fear that the same feelings will be hers someday. Down deep, she expects to be just like you.

Sometimes we set ourselves up for attack from our daughters by criticizing or punishing our own bodies. I'm still working hard at learning not to say negative things about my own old, hardworking body that has given me so much joy. This isn't easy, but raising my daughters has helped me in this, because bad feelings about my body are not a legacy I want to pass on. How, when I look at them, can I imagine it would be okay for them to disdain their own precious bodies—and therefore, how can I disdain mine?

We moms can be a great help to our daughters by talking about our bodies in positive ways. We can make every effort to talk about our bodies from the inside out—how it feels to exercise, to eat well, to rest and have energy, and so forth—as opposed to how we look from the outside in. We should also see a nutritionist or counselor if we need help with this issue. By getting the support we need for ourselves, we help our daughters avoid long-term struggles with food and body size.

What If You Said . . .

If your daughter has made a snide remark about your body, let her know you heard her, but without overreacting. Sometimes a little humor helps.

What? And all this time I thought I was perfect!

Ouch. That hurt a little. I am sensitive about my weight. I think you know that.

I would feel better and have more energy if I lost a little weight. Maybe I'll talk to a nutritionist about that.

I don't tease you about things you're truly sensitive about, and I expect the same courtesy from you.

"You Embarrass Me!"

*Why are our daughters so intensely
embarrassed by us—and we by them?
What can we do to relieve that anxiety?*

---

*I am half Chinese, and my mom is from China.
Once at dinner I sang a song about Chinese people's eyes
being slanty. I really hurt my mom's feelings. I do not
even know why I sang the song. I apologized to my mom
and that made me feel better. She pointed out that
not only was I making fun of her, I was also
making fun of myself.*

—Victoria, age 9

*When Izzy was 13, she would criticize me in front of my
friends. She would dredge up the most awful things—like
my weight and a guy I had cared about who decided to
marry someone else—deeply personal things. She was
very good at hitting below the belt. But now she's 16, and
she sent me a card last Mother's Day. It said, "No matter
how many times I've said mean things to you, I truly love
you and always will." I carry that card everywhere with
me in my purse. That's how much it means to me.*

—Lynne, mother of a 16-year-old girl

When your daughter began to speak, she said your name. When she took her first steps, they were to you. When, as a little girl, she imagined the worst, it was that you might leave her. Now at age 8 or 10 or even 12, she is still deeply connected to you, so much so that she has to struggle mightily to disentangle her identity from yours. In fact, that's her job as an adolescent—to become an individual, loved and supported by you but not part of you. How do we parents know our daughters are on task? That's easy. Our cars, our hair, and our clothes humiliate them. The fact that we breathe, speak, and walk around on the same planet with them is embarrassing almost beyond bearing. In other words, they're taking shape as individuals right on schedule.

My own parents were unbelievably embarrassing to me when I was a preteen. I used to lie down in the backseat of the car in hopes no one would know I was with them. Today, however, I have sympathy for any parent stung by a daughter's embarrassment. It can hurt deeply when the girl you love stiffens at your touch or slips out of your orbit whenever the two of you are in public. When my own 13-year-old begs me not to talk to her friends, I take comfort in the advice of psychologist Evelyn Bassoff. "It is the *parent* part of you, not the human part, she has to push away," Bassoff says.[1]

1. Evelyn Bassoff, "Family Life," in *What I Wish You Knew: Letters from Our Daughters' Lives, and Expert Advice on Staying Connected* (Pleasant Company Publications, 2001): 61.

Your daughter's rejection feels personal, but it's mostly developmental. She loves you as much as ever, but she is changing.

> *Once I said, "Mom, you're embarrassing me! Don't walk*
> *me to school any more!" I yelled at her for that because the*
> *other kids were laughing at me for being a baby, having to*
> *walk to school with my mom . . . Later I realized that it*
> *hurt my mom and that she just wanted me to be okay. I*
> *went up to her and said, "Mommy, I'm sorry. Let's walk to*
> *school early tomorrow. We'll go the long way." That did it!*
> —*Cindi, age 10*

Cindi's story is to the point. Her embarrassment was acute, but rejecting her mom was painful, too—for both of them.

The End of Adoration

The first hint of "parental" embarrassment usually shows up when a girl is eight or nine years old. At first, she is hardly conscious of it, yet it keeps surfacing—a niggling discomfort, the faint realization that she no longer feels the unquestioning adoration she used to feel for you. So she takes a gentle jab or makes jokes at your expense. Perhaps you'll forget something and she'll say, "That was stupid. Oh—just kidding, Mom." You'll both laugh, yet something shifts in the relationship. She still needs to be close to you, but she sees your imperfections and can't keep from voicing this confusion.

> *I said to my mom, "You look funny with that thing on." But*
> *I didn't really mean it, I think, and I was just being funny.*
> *I said I was sorry and I loved her and gave her a kiss.*
> —*Autumn, age 9*

Notice how ambivalent Autumn's feelings are about her mom. Her "I think" reveals her own confusion. If, like Autumn's mom, you're being treated with "come here, go away, come here, go away" behavior, your daughter is probably between seven and ten years old.

A year or two later, when a girl is ten or eleven, her embarrassment about and criticism of you may become more pronounced. An increasingly social creature, she may instruct you about what to wear and how to behave so as not to humiliate her (and, she feels, *yourself*). Hyperaware of how others perceive her, she is striving to become the star of her own drama, a girl who exerts some measure of control over her own life, and this requires that we parents slip into supporting roles.

> *One time I told my mom that I didn't want her to watch me in a karate competition. She hadn't done anything to make me mad. It was like I just didn't want her where everyone would see her. I know it must have hurt her to know that I wanted her to leave.*
>
> —*Shannon, age 11*

Pushing Us Away with More Strength

The deepest embarrassment often surfaces when a girl is 12 or 13 years old—those years that mark the apex of change. She walks the line between being a child able to do very little on her own and being a teen able to do so much on her own. At this point, her lingering attachment to you, the purest reminder of her dependent childhood, can cause overwhelming embarrassment, so she feels compelled to push you away with more strength. It's hard to know what will set off the stiffened body, the wide-eyed, horrified stare, and the hissed "Stop it, Mom" of an embarrassed girl. And it's difficult to respond with grace and without anger or sadness.

> *One time my friend and I were sitting by the pool and my mom came and sat next to me. I said, "Bye, Mom!" and she just walked away, but she looked sad.*
>
> —*Leigh Ann, age 13*

My goal these days is to remember that my daughter's actions and her words are often driven by the internal workings of her development. I very much want to avoid the deeper cuts and harsher criticism I know is possible between her and me. So, if I think to ask, I'll say, "Do I look okay?" before we go out together—not because I worry very much about how I look but as a show of respect for her feelings, which I hope will be returned. In particular, I ask before I wear my flowered pedal pushers out in public ("They're 'capris,' Mom, and, no, don't wear them."). I try not to answer the phone in that weird way that bugs her, and I am learning to stop talking to myself so much when I drive.

In the end, these are small concessions to a girl who, at this age, feels her identity so keenly threatened. Besides, it won't last long. Someday, when she's an older teen, she'll feel certain enough of who she is and separate enough from me that if I make a fool of myself, she'll actually hurt for me and not so much for herself. That will mark a passage indeed.

"NO OFFENSE, MOM, BUT . . ."

Girl: *(looking at herself in mirror)* *I so want contacts when I turn 11. You said I could have them then.*

Mom: *Yes, I did.*

Girl: *(with a sly look at her mother, who wears glasses) Besides, glasses are so geeky. Umm, no offense, Mom.*

What Just Happened?

The girl above is probably eight or nine years old, and she's making a typical first foray into embarrassment/insult territory. Make no mistake: this is a test. This girl's "slip" about glasses translates to "I don't automatically adore everything about you anymore." If the mom reacts in a way that says, "Of course you don't. I wouldn't expect you to," the two of them will probably move through this stage without too much trouble. But if the mom protests too much, the girl will feel developmentally driven to express her differences from her mom with more abrasive words.

Girls criticize their dads in this way, too, letting them know that they're no longer perfectly esteemed. A girl's harshest criticism, however, is usually reserved for her mom—the parent of the same sex who, without even trying, threatens a girl's sense of herself as unique.

When your daughter looks in the mirror, she sees a girl utterly unlike any other, a girl with unlimited potential, a young person who could grow up to be an exciting, adventurous, and wonderful woman. Then she looks at her mother, the person more similar to her than anybody else in the whole world, and she sees an impossibly flawed woman. It's embarrassing to be inextricably linked to such a mother! In order for our daughters to imagine and create the women they will become, they must, in effect, move us out of their way. Inevitably, they will utter words of criticism. Even if we understand what's happening, their criticism hurts.

This is one of those times when we're reminded that parenting is an uneven business. We are challenged to respond to this particular bit of developmental nastiness with restraint and respect, because that's what we want in return, and because our daughters are vulnerable to us in ways we will never be vulnerable to them. Their criticism of us stings, but our disapproval of them has the power to crush (even if our glasses *are* geeky).

What If You Said . . .

When she first begins to test you with mild insults, react as mildly as you are able.

Act as if you hardly noticed.
No offense taken. Glasses are geeky, but contacts are more trouble.

Let her know that you saw what she did, but that it doesn't bother you much.
It's natural, I guess, for girls to criticize their moms sometimes. I'm sorry you don't like glasses.

Acknowledge your sensitivity, and let her know you expect respect.
I know you're bound to feel critical of me in some ways, but I do appreciate your being respectful. I try not to criticize things that I know you feel sensitive about.

Try humor:
Oh no, I'm geeky! And all these years I thought I was devastatingly gorgeous!

"I CAN'T BE SEEN WITH YOU LOOKING LIKE THAT!"

Mom: *I'm ready. Where are my car keys?*

Girl: *Mom, you can't wear that dress again. It looks like a bag.*

Mom: *Don't start with me. I look fine.*

Girl: *No. I will not go with you wearing that. It's ugly. And can't you do something with your hair?*

Mom: *My hair looks like it always looks.*

Girl: *No, it's worse than usual today. Honestly, that's a terrible cut, and that color you put on it is all wrong.*

What Just Happened?

There's quite a difference between the "Oops, did I say that?" slight and an outright attack. The girl above is crossing that line. At some level, and probably for reasons she cannot articulate, this daughter is actually *afraid* for her individuality. Maybe her mom seems a little too close, the boundary between mother and daughter a little too permeable. Maybe the family situation is changing or tenuous. Maybe she has lost a friend or has been gossiped about at school. In any case, she has lost her psychological footing, and she's taking it out on her mom. This girl is to be pitied (growing up is painful), yet you and I cannot condone such attacks. In fact, our daughters depend on us to keep them from crossing the line into abusive language and behavior.

Meanwhile, we're bound to feel this attack at a visceral level. How could we not? Being deliberately targeted by the girl we love is a shock to both our bodies and our hearts. At this point, we need words and actions that buffer us against our daughters' battering words. That way, we won't be tempted to engage and batter back.

After all, the exchange above doesn't really qualify as a conversation. The girl isn't offering information as much as she is exercising her self-assertion and patrolling the fence line between herself and her mom. Something is going on inside her, and her mom may have no idea what it is. Fortunately, she doesn't have to know in order to respond in ways that soothe rather than challenge.

No matter what the root source of her criticism is, a daughter on the attack is looking to you to reassure her of your continued love for her despite her attempts to drive you away. She wants to admire you, but she has to test you. Good luck on the exam. Most of us have to take it more than once, but it gets easier with practice.

What If You Said . . .

When her embarrassment mounts and she attacks you, look for words that give you a buffer from her criticism and that reestablish mutual respect.

I had no idea the disaster was so complete! Help! Fetch my stylist!

When you speak to me in that tone, it puts me on the defensive. Can you make your request in a way that's easier for me to hear?

I will change my dress out of respect for your embarrassment about it, but it will help if you rephrase your request in a more considerate way.

Do you really want me to answer anything you've said? What is it that you want to have happen now?

I have a feeling this is not just about my dress and my hair. Do you know what's bothering you down deep?

I'm not really interested in going on an outing with you anymore. I love you, but your company is hard for me to deal with right now.

"BYE, MOM!"

Mom: *(in the kitchen when her daughter comes in with a group of girls) Hi, guys. What's happening?*

Daughter: *We're just getting some snacks and then (signaling with widened eyes to her friends) we're outta here. (To a friend) Here, take this bag of chips.*

Friend: *Hi, Ms. Bishop.*

Mom: *Hello, Ellen. What's new with you?*

Daughter: *(pulling her friend away) Let's go, everybody. Up to my room. (with emphasis) Bye, Mom!*

What Just Happened?

The same girl who still wants you to tuck her into bed may find your presence intolerably embarrassing when she's with her friends. Even if she still tells you all her secrets, she may insist you walk half a block behind or ahead of her when her peers are around.

Adolescent girls have to seek their own society at this age. Establishing herself among her peers is part of being an adolescent. Her brain structure plays a role, too. It may help you to know that in many instances, your daughter's senses are swamped with input when she is with her friends. Unlike our sons, who are likely to be more channel- and task-oriented in their thinking, our daughters tend to be extremely sensitive to all the signals people around them are sending. Your daughter is taking in all the nuances of how others are reacting to what's going on. In fact, researchers have found that girls consistently have a harder time than boys detaching themselves cognitively from their surroundings. Body postures, tones of voice, and facial expressions register with girls constantly.

When friends are around, a girl has lots of information to process already. Add a mom or a dad to the picture, and she has to monitor her friends' reactions to her parent as well. Her agitation and stress level rise, sometimes beyond bearing. She'll remove you from the equation if she can, if for no other reason than to relieve some of the intensity she feels.[2]

Being sent "back off" signals can make us parents—who remember the days when our daughters wanted to introduce us to all their friends—a little lonely. Yet it's a signal not that we're losing our daughters, but simply that they're growing up.

What If You Said . . .

If your daughter is embarrassed by you in front of her friends, look for a private time to express your understanding for what's going on and your confidence in your underlying relationship.

I remember how embarrassed I used to be when my friends saw me with my parents. One time my dad embarrassed me so much that I . . .

I know you need time with your friends, so I understand if you don't want me to be around when you're with them. But I appreciate your being polite about that and using kind words when you need me to leave.

I know it can be embarrassing to have parents around when your friends are over. That's the way it is with most parents and girls. I'll try to blend into the background—and that will save us both from embarrassment.

2. Helen Fisher, *The First Sex* (New York: Random House, 1999).

"YOU TALKED ABOUT ME BEHIND MY BACK"

Girl: *Mom, I heard what you told Kelly's mom on the phone yesterday. You talked about me behind my back.*

Mom: *You sound upset. What did I say?*

Girl: *You told her I wasn't any good on piano. You lowered your voice, but I was in the dining room and I could hear you.*

Mom: *Oh, dear. I didn't mean to hurt your feelings. I was talking without really thinking about what I was saying.*

Girl: *I'm used to it. You never think I'm any good at anything, and you tell all your friends how bad I am!*

Mom: *For heaven's sake, stop being so sensitive!*

What Just Happened?

The world in which our daughters live is filled with other kids who feel free to evaluate and ridicule them. So with us, our daughters ought to feel safe from that sort of hurt. Keeping trust with our daughters and respecting their privacy is of supreme importance. We parents, however, often need the insight and support we get from talking to other parents. Can we talk with friends about our daughters without betraying their trust? I think so. Here's how.

First, we have to be careful to share information about our daughters that's more or less "public" but respect their need to keep some things—especially the failings that embarrass them most—private. Certainly, we should never talk about things that we've promised our daughters we wouldn't discuss with anybody else. The amount of detail we share makes a difference, too. It's more of a betrayal to broadcast specific information such as "She made a D on a test," and less harmful to say something general like "She has to work hard in biology."

That said, any time we talk about our daughters with tenderness, we're probably on safe ground. You can feel within yourself the difference between a judgmental "She's impossible!" and an understanding "When we disagree, it's hard on both of us." The girl who overhears the second statement knows that you are still her ally.

What If You Said . . .

If your daughter calls you on the carpet for something you've said about her, try saying something like this:

I'm sorry. I shouldn't have said that. I love to talk about you, both your struggles and your successes. I'll try to be more careful from now on.

I'm sorry I hurt your feelings by talking about you. I know that you work hard at piano and that you're going to be really good if you keep at it.

We mothers have to talk to each other—that's part of being a mom. But the trust you and I have in each other is more important than anything. I'll try not to be critical of you to my friends anymore.

"YOU CAN'T WEAR THAT!"

Girl: *(singing) Over the river and through the 'burbs, to grandmother's house we . . .*

Dad: *What on earth are you wearing? You can't go to your grandparents' house in low-cut jeans. And they're skin-tight. Go put on something decent.*

Girl: *Hey! I wear them other places.*

Dad: *But not today. Go change!*

Girl: *Why?*

Dad: *CHANGE! NOW!*

What Just Happened?

Embarrassment can render us amazingly inarticulate with our daughters. The dad above loves his daughter and feels closely connected to her. Therefore, he would be embarrassed if she appeared before *his* parents in *those* jeans. After all, what would they think about him as a father if she did?

Girls fear we'll embarrass them in front of their friends, and we parents often have a similar fear. We want our daughters to make us look good in front of our friends, associates, and families; and we *really* want them to shine in front of our own parents—people who grew up in a more formal age and who have high expectations of us as parents. Thus, even if we can tolerate our daughter's low-cut jeans on a school day because every other girl in her grade is wearing them too, a different standard applies when she steps outside her world and into ours.

Explaining this in a way your daughter can accept is a challenge. She still thinks mostly in black and white. In her mind, when a thing is right, it's right, no matter what the circumstances. She may stand on the principle of the thing—"I'm the same person no matter what I'm wearing" or "My grandparents love me no matter what I wear!"—and it's hard to argue with the logic of that.

So don't. Appeal to her feelings instead. Ask her to be considerate of your embarrassment and of her grandparents' feelings. Ask her to take the high ground so the old folks will feel better. **Finally, think six months ahead. Will your embarrassment, no matter how intense, really matter then?** That thought may help you put her low-cuts—and maybe her nose ring and pink hair, too—in perspective.

What If You Said . . .

When you feel embarrassed about how your daughter looks, logic probably won't serve your cause. Talk about feelings instead, and look for compromises.

I know you wear those jeans to school, but this is a different setting, and I need to ask you to be considerate of the feelings of the people in this setting.

I know this sounds silly, but I get embarrassed by some of the things you wear. I used to embarrass my parents, too, when I wore my hair long in the sixties. Please respect my feelings on this occasion and change into some clothes that won't embarrass me.

This is one of those times when we need to compromise. Could you wear something less revealing to the dinner at your grandparents'? Later in the day, you could change into your jeans.

How you look matters to me. I feel that it reflects on me, even though you may feel that it doesn't.

"YOU WERE INCREDIBLY RUDE"

Mom: *There's Elaine. She's a friend of mine from breakfast club. Stand up straight. I'll introduce you.*

Girl: *(slouching pronouncedly) Don't bother.*

Mom: *Here she comes. Hi, Elaine! Good to see you. (hugs her friend) This is my daughter, Christie.*

Friend: *(extending her hand) Good to meet you. I think a lot of your mom.*

Girl: *(crossing arms, looking away) Right.*

Friend: *(exchanging an amused look with the mom) Well, I'm on errands. See you soon. (leaves)*

Mom: *What's wrong with you? You were incredibly rude. How am I supposed to explain your behavior next time I see her?*

What Just Happened?

We all feel embarrassed when our daughters don't make an effort to be polite to our friends or associates. We're just as embarrassed by this situation as they are when we do something that draws attention to ourselves in front of their friends.

If this is an isolated incident, you can assume that, like many kids, your daughter isn't comfortable handling adult interactions yet. Role-playing can help her know what you expect. Even a girl who used to be gracious to adults can go through a period of shyness and uncertainty, especially around age 11 or 12. The spotlight falls on her, and her adrenaline surges. Her heart pounds. She withdraws, appearing rude.

Other girls this age simply may be so absorbed in their own concerns that it doesn't register that they're being extremely impolite. If a girl repeats this kind of behavior often, you'll have to assume it is intentional, and you'll need to make your expectations very clear. You may even have to impose consequences if it becomes an ongoing problem. With most girls, however, a gentle reminder of your expectations does the trick. Baseline trust on our part is important, too. Our daughters often manage encounters with other adults better when we're not around to embarrass them!

What If You Said . . .

Be clear about your expectations and your feelings when she is rude, but be sure to express understanding and trust.

It was embarrassing to me that you didn't look Elaine in the eye and say hello. Let's do some role-playing when we get home so that you'll know what adults expect when they're introduced.

Was that intentional? Did you realize how rude you were?

That looked very hard for you, and it was embarrassing for me. What's going on? Are you feeling shy these days?

You know, other adults tell me you talk to them politely. But that's not true when I'm around. Are there things I can do that will make it easier for you to talk to my friends?

Measuring Up

In this competitive world, how can you support your daughter's efforts to excel, yet be clear that you love her because of who she is, not what she achieves?

I was once working on a science project and getting stressed out. I didn't know how to do something, and my parents tried to help. They gave suggestions, but I was too mad. I screamed at them and said they were completely wrong. Later, I realized what they had said made sense.

—Ameliana, age 12

When I was a kid, my parents always let me know—with words, a look, or by hitting me—that whatever I did, I should have done better. Then, last year, I kept getting angry at my ten-year-old. One day I was yelling at her— this little kid who had made some dumb mistake. I was yelling something like, "Can't you ever get that right?" She was backed into the corner with her shoulders pulled up around her ears. All at once I understood what was happening to her. So I got counseling and started to change the things I say to her. And I wrote a Kids' Bill of Rights and put it up in the kitchen. It says both girls have the right to be respected and the right to make mistakes.

—Robert, father of girls ages 8 and 10

You've seen your daughter do something well—hit a tennis ball, ace a spelling test, climb a rock wall, or sing with a chorus. You've watched the amazing process by which she uses those achievements like building blocks to shape her sense of self. At a fundamental level, she recognizes, "This is who I am: a girl who can do *this*," and in the process she changes, grows, and becomes. Achievement is important throughout our lives, but never more than during late childhood and early adolescence, when a girl actively assembles the many parts of her adult personality.

Your daughter's achievements at this stage of her life, and your support for those achievements, can actually change the course of her life. As your daughter leaves childhood, her brain goes through a developmental zenith. When she is 10 and 11 years old, her frontal lobes expand almost as fast as they did when she was a baby. After age 12, this growth spurt ends and a process called *pruning* begins. During pruning, the neural pathways a girl uses remain, but unused ones are discarded. This means that the skills your daughter develops now—arts, music, languages, team or individual sports—establish mental abilities that will stay with her into adulthood. They help shape what she can do and who she will be.[1]

1. *Nature Neuroscience* 2 (October 1999). Includes UCLA research on cycles of expansion and pruning seen in children's brain scans. A summary is in the *Washington Post,* March 9, 2000, article "Key Brain Growth Goes On into Teens."

Your support and understanding during these years are critical to your daughter. If a girl grows up feeling that her performance is good enough—that she can set goals, play or work hard, and know that the heart she brings to her efforts is supported and valued by you—she can pull her shoulders back and enter adulthood believing in herself. But if a girl grows up without that acknowledgment and appreciation from you, she cannot help but feel inadequacy and even shame. She lacks deep-rooted confidence. Her self-talk (the way she talks to herself about herself) becomes negative, and as a result she becomes more likely to fail.

Speaking with Compassion

Supporting a girl's hard work and achievement sounds simple, but it's not. Finding compassionate, encouraging words to say and ways to act is a challenge. When American Girl polled girls about hurtful words they had heard from their parents, one in every four stories the girls told was about grades and sports. One typical story:

> *Once I was just finishing up a ballet class, and my dad came at the end to watch. When we got to the car, he told me that I needed a lot of work on my dancing and that I wasn't the skinniest girl in the class. That really hurt me. I knew I wasn't the thinnest, but I was one of the best. I was really sad.*
>
> *—Emma, age 12*

This dad wants his daughter to succeed, but he is responding to his fear for her—that in this highly competitive world his daughter will not be skilled or distinguished enough to make her mark.

He feels tremendous anxiety about his daughter's performance.
Clearly, he is not alone. Every time a girl's grades come home,
every time her team plays in a tournament, every time she stands
in front of a crowd, you and I share her performance stress. In our
very bones, we ache for her to do well. Yet such anxiety can drive
us to say words to our daughters that convey debilitating pressure
and shame.

Think of this chapter as a mirror of chapter 4, "You Embarrass
Me!" There, we talked about girls' efforts to define themselves as
being different from us. When we push and punish girls regarding
their achievement, then *we* are the ones experiencing anxiety and
embarrassment, because we don't understand that our daughters'
achievements are not our own. It is one thing to be proud of a girl
and to provide her with the resources she needs in order to excel,
but it's quite another thing to become so involved that we take
credit or feel blame for her performance. If we get hung up on
competition, we lose sight of compassion.

> *One night I was baby-sitting in the biggest house in town,*
> *and I kept calling my mom because I was so scared that*
> *someone was going to break in. My parents and the parents*
> *of the girl I was baby-sitting had gone out to eat together,*
> *and my mom said, "You don't need to call so much, or*
> *they'll think you're scared and they won't ask you to sit*
> *again!"*
>
> —*Leah, age 11*

It's understandable that this mom was embarrassed in front
of her friends when her daughter failed to live up to everyone's
expectations. But by focusing on this girl's performance over her

emotional needs, this mom treated her as an object rather than an individual, a product rather than a person. Fortunately, that's a trap we parents usually can avoid.

It sounds contradictory, but compassion comes from clarity about our separateness from our daughter's achievements, about the fact that a girl's successes and failures are her own, and about the fact that we'll be there for her with baseline understanding and love, whether she wins or loses. We'll pick her up and dust her off when she falls, hug her tight, and send her back into the race with the kind of self-confidence that only we, the adults who love her most, can give her.

"I DON'T WANT YOUR HELP!"

Girl: *This social studies map is stupid. It doesn't make any sense!*

Dad: *Here. Look at the instructions again. You're not paying attention to what the different colors mean.*

Girl: *Yes, I am. This is useless. You aren't explaining it the way my teacher does. I hate social studies. Why do I have to study geopolitical spheres of influence anyway?*

Dad: *If you'll just calm down and listen to what I'm telling you, you'll learn something for a change!*

Girl: *Who asked you to butt in anyway?*

Dad: *You did! But now I'm so mad, I can hardly see straight.*

Girl: *Fine! I don't want your help!*

What Just Happened?

When a girl begins to get overwhelmed academically, the first place the stress shows up is in her homework. Just as academic pressure has increased on our daughters, so has the homework load—in fact, it has more than *tripled* since you and I were in school. A girl who has trouble with homework probably recognizes that she's not up to speed in the classroom. If she asks you to help, she may be fearful and defensive before you even sit down.

Offering to help can be problematic, too. When you say, "Do you want me to help?" she may hear, "I don't believe you can do this on your own." Given this prickly situation, a light touch is best. Educators suggest that before plunging in, you spend some time observing a girl who seems overwhelmed. Does she organize her work? Which tasks take a very long time? Does she know how to read for the big ideas and how to prioritize tasks? It may be best to talk with her about what has to be done first, what will take longest, when to take breaks, and so forth. If you do help her with specific assignments, go slow and easy, assuring her that you are certain she can do this on her own with just a little nudge from you.

What If You Said . . .

When you help your daughter with her homework, be alert to the feelings she may be having.

I know it's hard to ask for help, but I'm glad you did.

Help me figure out what you need most right now. Do you need to talk about how difficult all this is, or do you need me to work some of these problems with you until you get the hang of it?

Maybe I can help you get your work organized, and then you can do most of it on your own. What's the most important thing to do? Let's do that first, so you won't have to worry about it later.

Tuning In to Her Channel

In "Raising Emotionally Intelligent Teenagers" (Harmony Books, 2000), authors Maurice Elias, Steven Tobias, and Brian Friedlander remind us to tune in to what emotional need a girl is asking us to fill before we help. Their acronym for the signals she may send is FLASH.

I need to save **F**ace.
Please **L**isten to me.
I am looking for an **A**rgument.
I need **S**upport.
I need **H**elp.

"THIS GRADE IS TOO LOW"

Mom: *How did you do on that science test?*

Girl: *(hanging her head) Terrible. And I studied hard!*

Mom: *What did you get?*

Girl: *(handing her mom a paper) Here.*

Mom: *You got a D, and this was a major test! That's too low. I expect better grades than this from you!*

Girl: *It was really hard for everybody. I couldn't keep it straight.*

Mom: *You weren't paying attention, that's what! From now on, I expect you to take your work seriously. I don't want to see any more grades like this one!*

What Just Happened?

Before you talk with your daughter about a low grade, consider some of the reasons she may have scored poorly.

She's faced with new kinds of thinking. During middle school, the kind of thinking a girl is required to do shifts dramatically. Instead of learning skills like reading and writing, she has to apply those skills to solve problems. That's a new level of cognitive challenge, and during fifth, sixth, or seventh grade, she has to make big strides academically. She may stumble.

She balances a busy and distracting social life. During middle school, our daughters may go through a phase when they put their friends first and their studies second. We need to remember that not all the important work our daughters are doing is academic. They are trying to figure out the answers to social questions—such as how they fit in and what they get energy from doing. Also, they may feel pressure not to appear too smart because, if they do, they will pay a price in popularity. If we can acknowledge these social struggles, it may help us talk about the schoolwork our daughters have to do.

Another reason for occasional low grades is that school really *is* harder than it used to be. Across the country, schools hold our daughters to higher standards than before, and standardized testing makes a girl's abilities and shortcomings much more measurable and visible. If she's typical, your daughter is already worried about college by sixth grade.

What If You Said . . .

When faced with a bad grade, express your confidence in your daughter as well as your concern for her struggle.

First, listen:

I worry when you get bad grades, so I need for you to explain to me what happened that caused this grade to be so low.

If she worked hard but didn't make the mark:

What would you do differently next time? or *Maybe I can help you get organized to study for the next test like this one.*

If she didn't study:

I know it's important for you to spend time with friends. It's also important to do your studies. How can we schedule your time differently so that you'll get your studying done?

If she is really stressed:

This is just one grade. There will be others, and in the end you'll do fine. I know you work hard, and I'm proud of you all the time. Nobody does everything right. That wouldn't be normal!

"YOU'RE NOT VERY GOOD AT THAT"

Girl: *(singing soulfully in backseat of the car)* *"So lately I've been wondering who will be there to take my place—"*

Mom: *That's enough for now, Zoey.*

Girl: *Just a minute. I want to sing this for the Spring Concert. (resumes singing) "When I'm gone you'll need love—"*

Mom: *Honey, stop!*

Girl: *Don't you like that song?*

Mom: *It's not the song. You're off-key. If you want to sing a solo, you'll need to work on your voice.*

Girl: *(dejected) You don't think I'm good at <u>anything</u>.*

What Just Happened?

Girls entering adolescence are extremely sensitive to anything adults say about their abilities. Every day, our daughters find ways to ask "Who am I?" of themselves and of other people. They look to parents to answer that question, so even the smallest thing we tell girls about themselves sinks in deep and takes strong hold.

> *Once I asked my dad what a peninsula was. He said, "You don't know?" That really hurt my feelings, because it made me feel stupid. I was never able to admit it, though.*
>
> —*Clarke, age 13*

As a girl leaves childhood, her "pretend" dreams of greatness drop away, and she is expected to demonstrate achievement. She needs to hear us say that we believe she can, with work, become an accomplished person. That sounds easy, but it's not. In fact, instead of becoming gentler with our assessments, we tend to become harsher during the adolescent years. Researchers who videotaped parent/child interactions over time observed that the number of times parents expressed negativity about their kids' abilities rose steadily while the kids were between the ages of 10 and 15.[2]

There are lots of reasons for this. Girls begin looking like adults at this age, and we expect more of them as a result. Because girls become more critical of *us* at this age, there's a higher likelihood that they will return our criticism; one seemingly constructive comment from a parent can start a back-and-forth battle. We parents also feel the overwhelming pressure of the culture to make sure our children are high achievers. That comes at a price, however, if we forget how sensitive our daughters are to everything we say about their talents.

What If You Said . . .

Try to reinforce your daughter's self-confidence as you gently guide her toward understanding where her talents lie.

I know you love to sing. I think it's great that you're singing with a choir so that you can begin to train your voice the way serious singers do. I know you can do that if you put your mind to it.

Nobody is a naturally great singer. It just looks that way on TV. All serious singers have to train their voices. It takes determination and discipline, and you have both.

Nobody is great at everything—that would be weird. We all have to figure out our best talents and decide what we'll work hard at and be best in. Those are hard choices.

2. Charlene C. Gianetti and Molly Sagarese, *The Roller Coaster Years* (New York: Broadway Books, 1997): 66.

"I'M NOT SURE YOU CAN DO IT"

Girl: *I'm going out for the basketball team. Shelly is trying out and Krystal and Hannah—all of us.*

Mom: *Weren't they all on the team last year?*

Girl: *Yeah. It will be so fun!*

Mom: *But you've never played basketball on a real team before. Don't you know how hard that is? I'm not sure you can do it.*

What Just Happened?

Our words—because we're the primary adults in our daughters' lives—have predictive power. If we tell our daughters they'll be successful, our attitudes and theirs make this outcome more likely. If we predict failure, that, too, becomes the case. At both conscious and unconscious levels, girls absorb what we parents believe and say about them. They make choices based on what we've told them they can and cannot accomplish.

We want to see our daughters succeed, so why might we plant scenarios of failure in their heads? According to Christopher Andersonn, a sports specialist and the author of *Will You Still Love Me If I Don't Win?: A Guide for Parents of Young Athletes* (Owatonna, MN: Taylor Publishing, 2000), we parents carry around our own fears of failure and unresolved emotions from our own years as kids. We don't mean to, but we impose those feelings on our daughters, most of the time without even realizing we're doing it. Usually we want to protect our girls from failing and being humiliated (an experience most of us had at some time as kids), and we also want to protect ourselves from the embarrassment of seeing our daughters try and fail in public.

Self-talk is what we tell ourselves about ourselves, and it's a critical part of having confidence and performing well. The words we parents say have so much power in our daughters' lives that they pass pretty much unfiltered into girls' internal self-talk tapes. For example, if you say, "This training is too hard for you," that's what your daughter will tell herself, and before you know it, she'll drop the training. But if you say to her, "This training is hard, but I can tell you're getting stronger," that's what she'll tell herself. Her internal tapes won't slow her down, and she will be set up to feel successful, whether she wins or not.

What If You Said . . .

If you fear your daughter will fail, and yet she wants to try, find words that promote positive self-talk about doing her best.

Basketball is a new sport for you, and it takes a lot of skill and practice to play on a team. But I've seen you work hard before. You're a girl who knows how to put her energy and her heart into something.

This is going to be a challenge. I'm proud of you for trying hard things. Do you know what you'll need to learn and practice before tryouts? Let's set some goals, and then we can figure out how to help you get ready to try out.

I love your courage. You try really difficult things. Let me know if I can help you prepare.

"GET IN THERE! CAN'T YOU SEE THE BALL?"

Girl: *(during a break in practice)* Dad, I wish you wouldn't yell at me during practice. It throws me off. I'm trying to listen to my coach.

Dad: *I'm just trying to help. I can see what you're doing wrong, and sometimes you can't. Besides, I don't yell that much.*

Girl: *(near tears)* It's so much pressure. It makes me feel bad, like I can't do anything right. The other girls all hear you, too.

Dad: *What's the big deal? Since when is good advice a problem?*

What Just Happened?

Your daughter's on the field. You're in the stands. The ball goes right by her. Your heartbeat accelerates, your adrenaline flows. Suddenly, you're on your feet yelling. We've all been there— anxious, excited, and with less control than usual over our words.

When our daughters are extending themselves, taking risks, and reaching for a new level of play and self-confidence, the words we say are critical. The pressure and fear a girl feels in such moments is enormous. Even if your daughter is a casual player, she feels some degree of anxiety when she competes. She puts expectations on herself, and she wants to do well for her teammates and coach. Even more importantly, if you're on the sidelines watching, she fears failing you. She wants to live up to your expectations and make good on all the time and money you've invested in her participation. She's under pressure already, and negative words only make it that much worse. **No matter how self-confident she appears, she is still the child, and you're the parent. At the most fundamental level of her being, she needs to know that you won't reject her if her performance isn't good.** Yelling

"What the hell is wrong with you today?" from the bleachers will
hardly reassure her.

When we use discouraging or even abusive language during
a practice or a game, we are usually treating our daughters the
way we were treated when we competed as kids. That's the pattern
we learned, so we pass it on—unless we change our ways. When
we do change, our daughters become happier and more confident
people.

Try to find words that let your daughter know you're proud of
her and her efforts, no matter what the outcome of the competition.
Your belief in her fundamental ability and value helps her grow up
feeling "good enough," as opposed to flawed. In the long run, that's
the greatest gift you can give her.

What If You Said . . .

Look for words that affirm your daughter's efforts and let her
know how proud you are.

*I know it's discouraging to hear negative things yelled at you when
you're trying your best. Forgive me for making that mistake.*

*I'm going to try yelling positive things instead of pointing out your
mistakes. Keep reminding me, okay?*

*My parents used to yell advice to me, so that's what I grew up
learning to do. It's a hard habit to break, but I will try.*

*I need to remember that you can play this game on your own, and to
realize that I'm not part of the game myself. I promise I'll work
on that.*

"STOP TELLING ME WHAT I DID WRONG!"

Dad: *(as he and his daughter pull away from the soccer field)*
Your passing was off today. What was up with that?

Girl: *I know. I kept passing way short.*

Dad: *I thought maybe you were winded or something. Was that it?*

Girl: *I don't know. Let's not go over it again. My coach already talked to me about it.*

Dad: *I just want to help. Those passes were way below your standard. And I think they may have cost the team more than you realize.*

Girl: *I realize! I realize, for God's sake! Can you just shut up and stop telling me everything I did wrong?*

What Just Happened?

It's probably the most common mistake parents make in youth sports—analyzing a girl's mistakes on the way home from the game. First of all, she already knows (and how!) everything she did wrong. She's painfully aware that she made her mistakes in front of a world of people, her coach, her teammates and their families, her friends, and, most of all, *you.*

When she was younger, she probably looked forward to reliving practices and games with you on the way home in the car. But as her age and her skill level increase, so does the pressure. Her new achievements are spaced further and further apart, with months of hard work in between. Using the car ride to offer feedback, even well-intentioned advice, may seem natural and convenient to you and me, but it's seldom that way for our daughters.

In the survey for this book, many girls reported that the car ride home is a tense time when they need to hear less from us parents. Sports experts agree. Caroline Silby, coauthor of *Games Girls Play: Understanding and Guiding Young Female Athletes* (New York: St. Martin's Press, 2000), reminds us that immediately after a game, a girl is physically and emotionally exhausted. She needs this time to process her performance on her own. She may feel really trapped in the car, stuck listening to our advice when she needs some peace very badly. Furthermore, if she doesn't listen or asks us to be quiet, we (who didn't get to talk with her during the game) are likely to feel rejected. Naturally, the tension builds.

What If You Said . . .

On the ride home, give your daughter time to herself. Praise her effort, celebrate with her if she wants to talk about how well things went, but be careful not to analyze her performance or the game's outcome.

I was really proud of you out there today. I know it was hard. I want to talk with you about how you played, but let's do that tonight or tomorrow after you've had some time to rest.

I know you need some time to decompress, so I won't talk about your performance. I just want you to know that I'm proud of you.

Mistakes don't matter. Playing hard matters. Getting better matters. And I see you doing that all the time. You're a great kid, and I'm proud of you. I know you probably need some downtime right now. Want to turn on the radio?

CHAPTER

Her Own Space

Is the state of your daughter's room a classic battle starter in your household? Maybe you're actually fighting about bigger issues, like boundaries, control, and trust.

When I told my mom I wanted a new room, I said it was to get more privacy away from her and my younger sister. When I said that, she looked hurt.

—Jamie, age 12

We seldom argue about anything else, but we do battle over her room. If her room is messy, I just can't let it go. I've tried everything—rewards, silence, cleaning it with her. The only thing I really wish I hadn't done was use guilt and shame. I say things like, "I'd be embarrassed for somebody to come over and see this" or "Do you think your friend would want to visit in a room this messy?" Her room really pushes my buttons.

—Nicky, mother of a 13-year-old girl

A girl goes through a mind-boggling transformation between the ages of 8 and 14—right before our eyes. She enters this period just having mastered cursive writing, and she ends it taking practice SATs. Concepts go off like fireworks inside her head; abstract ideas such as justice and integrity suddenly have meaning. She begins reading the newspaper and big, fat books. Best of all, she gets your jokes. This is classic girlhood, and it's nothing short of amazing.

Where does all this development happen? At the dinner table, of course. In the classroom, online, at church or synagogue, and, most of all, in the privacy of her room.

In her room, she can spend hours lying on the bed, reading, daydreaming, and processing the experiences she needs to make sense of. This is where she makes up her mind about important issues and shares secrets with friends, where she checks out her changing body, practices kissing the pillows, and rehearses her basketball techniques in her head. This is where she relives her victories and worries about her shortcomings. Her room is also the sanctuary she retreats to after you and she have words. It's where she goes to cry or sulk, figure out what went wrong, and pull herself back together.

All these everyday acts require privacy. In fact, growing up itself is a process that requires privacy. That's why a girl's room is so important to her. It is the safe haven (sometimes the only haven she has) where she can be alone with herself. There she discovers the person she is growing up to be.

If you've never thought about the role your daughter's room plays in helping her mature, you're not alone. There is almost always a lag between the speed with which a girl assumes owner-ship of her room and the rate at which parents recognize her need for ownership and privacy.

It's understandable that we parents are slow on the uptake. When our daughter was a little girl, we were completely respon-sible for seeing that her bedroom was safe, inviting, and clean. But as soon as our daughter entered grade school, ownership of her room began to shift subtly. By age seven or eight, a girl has her own ideas about how her room should be decorated and whether or not it needs to be straightened. A girl this age accumulates the debris of her life away from home—school projects, party favors, borrowed clothes, and sports equipment—and this piles up in her room. By the time a girl is ten, she keeps a diary and e-mails her friends. In short, she does what she's supposed to do—claims appropriate areas of privacy as she creates an active life that is increasingly her own. The epicenter of this enormous shift is her room.

What the Mess Means

A mess in a girl's room is a sign that she owns, or needs to own, the space. Girls who live in neat houses tend to have messy rooms, but girls in messy houses often have well-organized rooms. A room that's not like the rest of the house says, "I'm me, and this is mine." That's usually a sign of what psychologists call healthy *individuation*, a signal that a girl is defining who she is.

Here's what her messy room *does not* mean. It *does not* mean she disrespects you. It does not mean you're an inadequate or overly indulgent parent. There are lots of household rules and regulations that matter a lot—such as her telling you where she is at all times, doing her homework, and not experimenting with cigarettes or alcohol. But the dirty clothes heaped on the floor, the old school papers piled in the corner on top of a pizza box (yes, it's not pretty) fall into another, and less critical, category altogether.

> *I used to be on Erin all the time to clean her room. Finally, I realized that the fights were not worth it. My definition of a clean room is very different from Erin's. Every month or so, I help her clean her room to my definition. The rest of the time she keeps it according to her standards. As long as there's nothing growing mold under her bed, I close the door and smile.*
>
> *—Liz, mother of a ten-year-old girl*

Big Issues, Big Emotions

Girls don't set out to betray us by growing up, but sometimes it feels that way. When a girl becomes less dependent than she used to be, it's easy for us parents to feel threatened. We're losing the child she used to be. Grief (sometimes disguised as anger) is a natural reaction. Arguments about our daughters' rooms are about much more than mess or organization. They're about loss, boundaries, control, trust, and letting girls grow up. That's why a messy room can drive otherwise reasonable parents to the edge. And any time our feelings are out of control, so are our words.

This subject is rough terrain (and a messy floor!), but we have to walk it. We can learn to affirm our daughters' newfound

---

Pack Rat Syndrome

Do you ever look at your daughter's room and think "pack rat"? An adolescent girl can be a ferocious collector. Beanie Babies, CDs, scrunchies, book series— all that *stuff* comforts her. If you're an adolescent and you keep changing all the time, surrounding yourself with your things helps you feel grounded. A collection of stickers on your wall or stuffed bears on your bed reflects back to you yourself. It gives you a way of asserting, "This is mine, and this is who I am. I'm the girl who likes these particular things."

Take heart. Now and then the pack rat does clean out her burrow. Your daughter is most likely to invite you to help pack up things and reorganize her room around transition times in her life such as the move to middle school or junior high, her bat mitzvah, or a trip to summer camp. No matter how "packed" the rat, be careful not to throw out or give away her things until she is ready to let go of them. A girl feels sadness about leaving childhood. Throwing out her beloved stuff only makes it worse.

---

maturity by respecting their tastes and tolerance for mess while we look out for their well-being and safety. Fortunately, all our hard work on this issue is time well spent, because it allows us to maintain loving relationships with our amazing daughters—these growing girls who give us hugs, who make us laugh, and who invite us to stay close when we give them the room they need to grow.

"HOW CAN YOU BE SUCH A SLOB?"

Mom: *What are you doing lying there reading? You're supposed to be cleaning up in here.*

Girl: *I will. Just let me finish this page.*

Mom: *Finish that page? You just don't get it, do you? I expect you to do what you've said you'll do, and clean your room!*

Girl: *Mom! You're making such a big deal out of a little mess! And besides, it's my mess, not yours.*

Mom: *That's right. Your mess in my house! This room is a pigsty. How can you be such a slob?*

What Just Happened?

If your daughter's room is a mess, what it signifies is that she's a kid in the process of growing up. Her room is the filled-to-the-brim container for all the activity, energy, confusion, and excitement in her life. Some girls are neat (God bless you, every one), but most are not. Therefore, we parents usually benefit from standing in the doorway of our daughters' rooms and trying hard to see those rooms as our daughters see them—as the places where the girls we love choose among all sorts of roles, activities, and ideas and put themselves together, repeatedly, in new ways.

You are right on target if you are paying close attention to the state of your daughter's room: it reflects the turmoil in her life. But mess itself is not the problem. On the contrary, it's typical, and it doesn't signal the despair or lack of focus it would likely signal in an adult's living space. Remember that mess in a girl's room, to her, is a sign that it's her own space, her territory. Take a deep breath and remind yourself that it does not mean you are a lax parent.

All the same, we feel the need for compliance from our daughters. We need to know that they pay attention to what we ask of them. The mom in this example is bothered by the mess but even more so by her daughter's dismissive attitude about what her mom wants her to do. No wonder we sometimes lose it and call a girl's room a pigsty and a girl a slob. Even so, name-calling and labeling don't get us results and are certain to damage the relationship. (See our discussion of labeling in chapter 2, "When Words Hurt.") A better approach is the compromise that gives your daughter control over the space but also garners you some respect from your daughter.

What If You Said . . .

If you've used harsh words with your daughter about her room, these words may move the conversation in a new direction:

I shouldn't have called you a slob. That had to hurt. But I'm upset because I expected you to have cleaned up in here by now, and you don't seem concerned about that.

I'm sorry I called your room a pigsty and you a slob. I lost it because I really feel offended by this mess. Can we find some way for your messy room to not be something we fight about all the time?

Your standards for cleaning up are totally different from mine. This room would drive me crazy, but I can see it's not that way for you. Why do you think it's so different for us?

You obviously are not going to straighten your room the way I would straighten it if it were mine. Maybe that's because you're a kid and I'm an adult. Would you promise to straighten in here every other Saturday, if I promise to leave you alone about it in between times?

"YOU HAVE NO TASTE"

Girl: *Mom, I don't like that blue bedspread.*

Mom: *But it's pretty, honey. And it looks great with your rug.*

Girl: *I told you I wanted purple, and I don't like the rug either. It has been in here since I was little.*

Mom: *It was bought for this room. It works in here. I'm not going to buy you a new rug.*

Girl: *I don't want one! Can't we just take it out of here? Then I won't need the bedspread either. I could use my old sleeping bag—the one with horses on it. That would look cool.*

Mom: *I don't think so! Can't you see that this bedspread is lovely? Honestly, you have no taste!*

What Just Happened?

Actually, this girl isn't *supposed* to have taste yet. She's a kid. These are the years when she tries out lots of looks and combinations to see what satisfies her nascent sense of the aesthetic (emphasis on *nascent*). Her tattered sleeping bag might not be beautiful to the mother, but this girl has a different measure for what "works." Besides, the sleeping bag is temporary. At age 7, she wants blue flowers and animal posters, but when she's 9 it may be Star Wars and basketball players. By age 12, it might be purple walls and rock bands.

When my daughter was 9, I helped her put her room together. We rearranged the furniture, packed up things she was ready to let go of, and went to buy fabric for new curtains. In a store, she found a loud (read *neon*) jungle print with jaguars on it. "Wow, it's on sale!" she shouted. "It wasn't selling very well," the salesperson

explained. "That," my daughter told her, "is because you don't
have enough kids shopping in here." Once a girl reaches a certain
age (somewhere between 8 and 11 years old), our adult aesthetic
doesn't feel right to her in her room. No matter how good our taste,
our daughters look at their rooms with their own eyes. They know
best what nurtures them and affirms them in the space where they
are most themselves.

In the end, it's not about decorating. It's about respect.
The girls we love control so little of their lives. They have to get up
when we tell them to get up, go to bed when we tell them it's time,
and eat at least some of what we put on the table. They have to go
to the schools and religious services we choose for them and obey
the rules we make to keep them safe. When we give them practice
making choices, we let them know we love them for who they are.
Decorating choices in their bedrooms are a natural place to start.

What If You Said . . .

What will you say when your daughter tells you she doesn't
like your decorating decisions? Here are a few suggestions:

*My first reaction is to be hurt that you criticized how I want things
to be, but I think you're trying to say something that seems
important to you. Sometimes I forget how much you're changing. Of course you're not going to like the same things I like.*

*I'm used to making all the decisions about how things look in our
house, but I can tell you don't want me to decide about this. Can
we split the difference somehow? What if you put your sleeping
bag on the bed, but the rug stays where it is?*

*This is something new—for you to make decisions about how your
room looks. Let me think about how important this is to me and
to you. Then we can talk again tomorrow.*

"GET OUT! YOU HAVE NO RIGHT TO BE HERE"

Mom: *(entering daughter's room) Dana, dinner is almost ready. Come set the table, please.*

Girl: *(stuffing her journal into a drawer) You did it again! You walked right in here without knocking. Knock! Knock before you enter!*

Mom: *What?*

Girl: *You have no right to come in here unless I say you can! This is my room.*

Mom: *Listen, young lady, as long as you're under my roof, I'll decide how much privacy you have!*

What Just Happened?

If you haven't begun knocking before you enter your daughter's room, it's probably time to start. Most school-age girls appreciate this show of respect, even if they still like to have you visit in their rooms or tuck them in at night. If you think about what goes on in a girl's room, you'll realize why every girl needs a warning when somebody is walking in on her. Your daughter writes in her diary in there. She studies her face in the mirror as she practices a flirtatious glance or lifting an eyebrow with disdain. She tries on outfits, puts on makeup, listens to music, dances with herself, and imagines how it will be to have romantic feelings.

A girl's room is her refuge. Where does she retreat to after you and she have words? Her room. There she nurses her grudge, realizes she was in the wrong, or waits for you to come and apologize if you need to. In her room, a girl expects to feel safe from the pressures of the world.

Various girls at various ages need differing amounts of privacy. Most girls begin closing their doors more often as soon as their bodies begin to change, and they expect you to knock before you go in. Dr. Linda Ashford, my co-author on this book, has one daughter who seemed to visit her room only to change clothes and sleep. Privacy was never a big issue. But Linda's younger daughter has always insisted on lots of privacy. Even as a little girl, she would ask her mom to stand in the doorway of her room and watch her play, but not to come in. This is an area in which each of us needs to follow our daughters' cues. They generally let us know how much privacy they need.

What If You Said . . .

If your daughter challenges your right to come into her room, try these words to calm the situation:

You do need privacy, but I need to be spoken to with respect. Can you make your request about knocking in a way that isn't so offensive?

Sorry, I keep forgetting. When you were little, you didn't mind if I walked in any time, so knocking is a new habit for me to learn. Let's try that again, and we'll both try to keep our tempers in check this time.

It's hard for me to find the right balance here, because this is your room, but it's inside our house. Please make your request in a more respectful way, and then we can talk about how much privacy you need these days. Let's talk in the dining room, so that we're not right in the middle of the space we're fighting about.

"YOU READ MY JOURNAL, DIDN'T YOU?"

Girl: *Dad! Somebody has been in my room. I can tell!*

Dad: *What do you mean?*

Girl: *My journal has been moved. It is in a different place than where I left it. I've told you I don't want anybody coming in here. Did Kelly come in here while I was gone?*

Dad: *Not that I know of.*

Girl: *Wait a minute. It was you, wasn't it? You read my journal!*

What Just Happened?

If you've ever been caught snooping, you know it's a hard situation to deal with. Almost anything you say will cause a blowup. In fact, if you've looked through your daughter's room, her diary, or her backpack just to satisfy your curiosity, you'll probably be hard-pressed to defend your actions. We damage our relationships with our daughters when we habitually distrust them.

When you're tempted to snoop, try talking directly to your daughter rather than playing detective. Trust your instincts. If you think something is wrong, it probably is, but unless your relationship is already strained, your daughter may be willing to tell you what's going on. At least give her a chance to do so.

If your daughter is in a jam of some sort, she may be looking for an opportunity to talk to you. If you're worried about what's going on in her life, make a point of spending time with her. (A road trip or a camp-out can get the talking started.) Ask her what's wrong, and keep asking. E-mail and notes work, too, especially for a girl who wants to tell you her problems but can't get the words out face to face. If you need to, remind her that you're a lot easier on a kid who tells you she has done something wrong than on a girl who hides her infractions. One question that can save lots of snooping is, "Is there any question you need to ask me that you haven't asked?"

That said, there are situations in which we must intervene because the stakes are so high. Has she stopped eating enough? Do you see signs of depression or alcohol use? Do people you don't know call her late at night? If you fear for your daughter's well-being, then reading her diary or looking through her room may be the only way to get the information you need to help her. Ask first, give her every chance to come clean, but snoop if you have to.

What If You Said . . .

If your daughter catches you snooping through her things, it may help to try words like these:

There probably isn't anything I can say that will justify my actions to you. I am sorry I snooped, but I'm not sorry that I worry about you and want to make sure I know what's going on in your life. I'm the person who can help you most if you are ever in any trouble. I love you so much that I never want anything bad to happen to you. That's why I keep a close eye on you.

Please forgive me for snooping this one time. I'm always going to worry about you because I'm your dad. And I am worried now. There's something I need to ask you about.

I have the uneasy feeling you may be making some choices that can get you into trouble. That's why I was snooping. I need to talk with you about . . .

I'm sorry I snooped, but I remember how hard it is to tell your parents things they need to know to keep you safe. And I'm a protective dad. I'll try not to snoop, but I need you to try to always talk to me about what's going on with you.

"DON'T YOU TRUST ME?"

Dad: *(standing outside his daughter's room) Honey, come out here. I need to talk to you.*

Girl: *(coming out, laughing) Just a minute, you guys. What's up, Dad?*

Dad: *Are Daniel and Jonathan in there with you and Kelly?*

Girl: *Yeah.*

Dad: *Why don't you all come down to the den or out on the porch? It's a nice day outside.*

Girl: *Not right now. We're online with Jason.*

Dad: *This doesn't feel right to me. I don't like it that there are boys in your room.*

Girl: *Dad, we're just hanging out. We're just buds. What's the matter? Don't you trust me?*

What Just Happened?

Don't you trust me?" is a loaded question, and if you haven't heard it from your daughter yet, you will during the next few years. It's good to have thought about your answer in advance. The first thing to do is to avoid the dead end "Yes, I do"/"No, you don't" argument, which is where most of us land the first time these words come up. **Instead of answering yes or no, talk specifically about the situation to which you object.** As always, be sure to talk about your fears or concerns rather than your daughter's shortcomings, and brainstorm with your daughter about ways she can relieve your worry.

Ann Caron, the author of *Don't Stop Loving Me: A Reassuring Guide for the Mothers of Adolescent Daughters* (New York: Henry

Holt & Co., 1991), recommends an approach she calls "vigilant trust." This kind of trust means believing that our daughters usually make good choices, yet at the same time staying aware of what's going on among their friends and peers. As parents, we can and often do see trouble coming before our daughters do. Vigilant trust means that you stay one step ahead by checking in with other parents and with your daughter's teachers so that you know what other kids her age are doing—whether or not they're smoking, for example, or are sexually active. Then you can talk specifically with your daughter about your concerns. Most girls don't mind this kind of vigilance if it's paired with basic trust.

What If You Said . . .

When your daughter says, "Don't you trust me?" try these responses to show that you are trusting, but vigilant:

I do trust that you have good intentions. I'm worried, though, that having boys up in your room puts you in a position where things can easily be misinterpreted or get out of hand. I can't feel good about allowing that.

I know Daniel and Jonathan are just your friends, and you hang out together. But I'm going to be much more comfortable about all of you if you hang out in some place that's not so private.

I don't want to embarrass you in front of your friends, but for now make sure you leave the door open. And after they leave, let's sit down and talk about some guidelines that would help us both feel okay about what happens when your friends visit.

CHAPTER

Crossing the Line

*She is trying to grow up and be venturesome,
but your job is to keep her safe. How will you
find the right words to negotiate the
many steps along the way?*

---

*One time my mom said that I couldn't go skating with my
friends on Sunday. Well, all of my friends were going and
I <u>really</u> wanted to go! After the tenth argument that day, I
said to her, "All my other friends are going. I wish
I had one of their moms!"*

—Justine, age 12

*Kate was determined to ride her bike to the park alone,
but I said she wasn't old enough. Later, I was sitting at
my computer when I heard her yelling from the front
yard. She was out there on the sidewalk with her bike,
yelling "I want to go!" She wasn't going behind my back,
thank goodness. And it hit me that she was attempting to
reopen the question in the best way she knew how. So I
tried to respect that and went out to talk to her. In the
end, she got to ride to the park, but with me shadowing
her a block or so behind.*

—Anne, mother of a nine-year-old girl

When our daughters are little girls, they tend to think like we think. They see us as founts of judgment and truth because that's what they need us to be. When we are clear about the rules, the world is a predictable place for our five- and six-year-old daughters, and they feel secure. But during the next few years, things change. Around age eight, a girl experiences a cognitive "click." Suddenly, math concepts make more sense to her, and she can construct an orderly sequence of thoughts about a fairly complicated subject. At this point, the little girl is gone, and a "kid" has taken her place—a girl with different needs when it comes to rules and limits.

> *We were riding an escalator in a department store when she said, "You know, Mom, everything you like, I don't like." It was new for her to say something oppositional like that. At first I wanted to contradict her and tell her we really liked a lot of the same things deep down. But somehow I knew that wasn't a good response. Finally I said, "Well, sometimes that's just how it is between daughters and moms."*
>
> *—Nancy, mother of a then seven-year-old girl*

Nancy remembers that comment as a signal. Something new had begun.

The Art of the Daughter Deal

When our daughters are between 8 and 14, we learn the art of walking the fine line between being tyrannical and permissive. During this stage, girls need their parents to be firm yet able to negotiate. Psychologists call this stance *authoritative.* As an authoritative parent, you approach each case with an open mind. You listen to your daughter's point of view, and sometimes you are swayed by her arguments. But once you render a decision, you hold firm.

Each of us negotiates every day—at work, with friends, and with family members. In the course of doing that, we've all learned many of the rules of good negotiations. These rules apply just as much when we talk with our daughters as they do when we're working out business solutions. Here are a few examples:

- *Take your time.* Don't expect to solve a difficult problem or work out a partnership with just one meeting.
- *Bring the standards to the table.* Talk with other parents to find out what the rules are in their families.
- *Ask questions* for as long as you need to—until you understand all the needs of the other side.
- *Use the word "fair" when you propose middle ground.* School-age girls have an intense sense of fairness and justice. If, for example, your nine-year-old daughter wants to stay up until 11:30 P.M. when her friends are over, but you want her in bed at 9:30, propose a compromise this way: "Let's try 10 o'clock. That feels fair to me." Simply introducing the word "fair" often has a calming effect on the conversation.
- *Be generous.* Throw in something you didn't have to concede. Leaving something on the table for the person you're negotiating with helps her feel better about the outcome.

Girls, Rules, and Words

Words are absolutely critical to the rule-setting process—especially when we're dealing with girls. After studying language differences between men and women, linguist Deborah Tannen concluded that women, more often than men, feel it is natural to consult with others about decisions; and this trait, she says, begins in girlhood. Girls routinely expect rules and decisions to be discussed before they're enacted, and they appreciate the discussion itself as evidence of connection.

This means that you and I get parent points each time we say "Tell me more," "I see your point," or "Convince me." Our willingness to listen to our daughters does not mean that we will compromise our values, but it does signal that we're willing to talk about middle ground, which gives girls a little more responsibility and freedom than they have had before.

Research shows that when we just hand kids rules without getting their input, they tend to turn to peers when they have problems or need support. But girls who know that their parents listen to their opinions are more likely to turn to them with problems.

The Power of Listening

Linguists observe that when girls and women talk, they tend to anchor their gaze on each other's faces, occasionally glancing away, while boys and men anchor their gaze elsewhere in the room, occasionally glancing at each other.[1] If you're negotiating a rule with

---

1. Deborah Tannen, *You Just Don't Understand: Women and Men in Conversation* (New York: Morrow Avon, 1990). While boys are often more likely to contradict another person verbally, they're less likely to do so in a face-to-face body stance. Girls tend to seek more mutual ground with their words and engage directly with gaze or body stance.

your daughter, she is more likely to feel that you are listening to her point of view if you make lots of eye contact. Let her sit facing you, too. That's the position girls and women most often choose when they're discussing something. Boys tend to sit parallel or at angles to each other.

In her book *The Difference: Discovering the Hidden Ways We Silence Girls—Finding Alternatives that Can Give Them a Voice* (Burbank, CA: Warner, 1996), author Judy Mann talks about listening respectfully to what girls have to say.

> . . . *By listening closely to my daughter and what she has to say . . . I realize I can give her something other than love, which comes with virtually no thought, no judgment, no holding back. I can also give her admiration and respect for how she thinks and how she handles herself. This requires me to stand head to head with my daughter and not look down upon her because she is young. . . . it requires me to see her as a person of accomplishment . . . not as a child who is merely a receiver of my mothering. As I look at her this way, my expectations of her take on a new dimension. They are less attached to me and more attached to her; they are disentangled from my emotions and more attached to her accomplishments.*

This simple act of listening has a powerful effect on parent and girl alike, and it transforms our approach to setting rules.

Living with Fear

In the midst of negotiating and listening, we parents also learn to live with fear. I cannot count the times I've waved one of my daughters off on some new adventure—crossing a busy street, going to a new school, or taking off for a wilderness adventure. My smile says, "Go, girl!" but inside I add a silent prayer—"and be careful!" From the instant our daughters are born, the world feels like a more dangerous place than it was before. Sometimes our concerns intensify when a girl hits puberty because her budding sexuality makes us worry that she's now more vulnerable. Before your ten-year-old rides her bike down the block, you assess the neighborhood, the time of day, the number of strangers on the street, the weather, and the speed of traffic. On top of that, you also have to assess your daughter's level of experience and good judgment. At ten, she is *supposed* to be testing some of the limits and discovering how it feels to be brave and confident—yet it's your job to keep her safe. That sounds like the proverbial "rock and a hard place" because sometimes it is.

In this chapter we'll explore finding the right words as we determine reasonable and safe rules and limits for our daughters. We'll talk about what it means to trust our own judgment at the same time we're listening carefully to the girls we love.

"YOU'RE SO MEAN!"

Girl: *Mom, I want to go to Sandra's house.*

Mom: *I don't think so. There's too much on the schedule today already.*

Girl: *Come on. Please?*

Mom: *I'd love for you to be able to go, honey, but I don't have time to drive you there or pick you up. There are other things I have to do.*

Girl: *You never let me do anything! You're so mean!*

What Just Happened?

Lots of girls retort "You're mean" when we refuse them something they want. "Your rules are stupid" or "You're not my friend" also apply here. Since the words aren't literally true, what do they mean? In the first place, "You're mean" indicates that your daughter has trouble thinking beyond *now*—partly because of her level of cognitive development and partly because, during this exchange, it's not in her best interest to think in a broader context. In that instant, she probably *does* feel that you are, indeed, mean. "You're mean" is also shorthand for "You've hurt me. Well, I can hurt you, too. So there."

"You're mean" is one of the first phrases our daughters use when they run afoul of the rules we set. Girls of seven and eight tend to use it. And, while the words may not be kind or true, neither are they abusive. More than anything else, "You're mean" is pure protest, and protesting is a useful skill for girls to have. In fact, we *want* our daughters to know how to protest so that, free to say what they think and feel, they grow up to be honest and direct. As parents, you and I are the people our daughters practice their new verbal skills on. Our ability to tolerate and even respect their protests (not their abuse or attacks, but their protests) teaches them that they have a right to have their voices heard.

What If You Said . . .

Y ou may not be able to convince your daughter that you aren't an ogre, but letting her know that you understand her feelings can help.

I'm not trying to be mean. I'm sorry that my decision feels that way to you.

I hear you. I know you're mad. I'm sorry that we can't change the schedule today.

It doesn't feel good to me, either, when I have to say no about something. But sometimes I have to. This is one of those times.

If you actually do have flexibility and can consider her request:

Let's brainstorm about this. If I drive you to Sandra's, you'll have to take something else off the schedule. Do you remember all the things we already have planned for today?

"JUST LEAVE ME ALONE!"

Girl: *I can too do soccer and basketball at the same time. You always say two sports is too many.*

Dad: *Don't you remember last year? You got really run-down with all those practices and games and homework, too. Just one sport per semester—that's the rule.*

Girl: *That was last year. I'm older now!*

Dad: *Don't you see that I'm just trying to help you manage your time—*

Girl: *Oh, just leave me alone! (storms out of the room)*

What Just Happened?

"Leave me alone" tells us a great deal about how a girl is feeling. Like a red light, it signals us to stop and give her a moment, because our instruction is more than she can stand just then. Or she might say "whatever," "back off," "chill out," or "I *got* it—okay?" Whichever phrase she uses, try to hear, "Don't tell me all those negative things right now. I don't want to hear them. I don't like the way you make me feel when you remind me of the realities of the situation."

Sometimes we pull in one direction and our daughters simply have to pull in the other. They feel ready to take on the world, but we constantly ask them to slow down and take one small step at a time. It can be useful to think of "Leave me alone" and other resistance as part of your daughter's job at this age—which is finding out what she is capable of doing. My youngest daughter is 13. Not long ago she said "Chill" to me when I asked for the second time if she had money for the bus ride home from the library downtown. "Chill" is older-kid shorthand for "Leave me alone." I did a quick internal burn, but then I reminded myself that she was just doing her job at that point, letting me know she felt she could handle this. That thought helped me find the right words sooner.

What If You Said . . .

Words like these can help encourage conversation when you've been summarily dismissed by your daughter:

I understand you need to end this conversation for now, but I wish you'd say it in a way that isn't disrespectful to me.

I'm not sure you'll be able to handle that situation. It must hurt you to hear me say that.

Okay, but I want us to talk about this some more later.

Let's both take some time to think about this. Maybe there's some way to reach middle ground that we haven't thought of yet.

"I'M NOT A BABY ANYMORE!"

Girl: *Mom, Dallas's mother says she can go to the rink for the skate-till-midnight party. Can I go, too?*

Mom: *Absolutely not. It's full of high-school kids in the evenings. It's too dangerous.*

Girl: *That's not fair. I'm in sixth grade! What am I supposed to do—stay home my whole life?*

Mom: *Don't exaggerate. Of course you're not going to stay home your whole life. But you're not going skating until midnight. I said no, and I meant it.*

Girl: *When are you going to stop acting like a baby-sitter and let me grow up? You never let me do anything!*

What Just Happened?

This conversation is packed with fear. The mom is afraid for her daughter's safety, and the daughter is afraid her mom isn't just protecting her but is controlling her life. Any time we give a knee-jerk "no" to a request that isn't overtly dangerous or inappropriate given a girl's age, our daughters fear that we don't trust them to grow up. We have to determine whether our daughters are legitimately pushing against boundaries that treat them as too young or if they are using "don't treat me like a baby" to get what they want.

If you hear phrases like "Stop being a baby-sitter" or "You treat me like a baby" regularly, it may be time to ask some questions about the rules you're trying to enforce. Ask yourself:

- *Do I know enough?* Have I asked enough questions so that I have all the information I need?
- *Are my fears justified?*
- *Have we tried problem solving yet?*

If the answers are yes, yes, and yes, then listen compassionately to your daughter's protests but hold firm to your decision. Even if you have to say no in the end, the time you spend exploring her request further will be well spent. Your willingness to listen and discuss the possibilities sets a tone and begins a dialogue that will serve you both for years to come.

Begin by searching for words that acknowledge your anxiety. Then use words that recognize your daughter's competence and growing ability to take care of herself. Finally, problem solve with her about ways she can stay safe. For example, in the scenario above, the girl might agree to go with a group of girls, carry a cell phone, and come home at nine. That's a win-win situation, because the daughter feels competent, and her mom gets to teach her ways of taking care of herself.

What If You Said . . .

Acknowledging your worry as your own is important. It lets your daughter know that you're aware of danger. Furthermore, it invites her to brainstorm ways of staying safe.

That makes me nervous. The skating rink gets really full and rowdy at those midnight parties.

Have you and Dallas talked about ways of taking care of yourselves there? Give me some examples.

Yes, you could take the cell phone, and what else? How about going with a bigger group of girls?

You've got some good ideas, but I still have to think about this for a day or two. It's a big decision.

"YOU ARE SO EIGHTIES"

Girl: *All the other girls have TVs in their rooms. Everybody in my class does.*

Mom: *Yes, but in our family we only need the TV in the den and the one in the kitchen. That's plenty.*

Girl: *But I <u>need</u> one in my room. Then I can watch stuff without disturbing you.*

Mom: *I prefer not having too many TVs. They get in the way of having family time together.*

Girl: *Nobody else in the whole world watches as little TV as you do, Mom! You are so eighties.*

What Just Happened?

If your daughter tells you you're old-fashioned or, by her standards, "so eighties," you can take several messages away from the exchange. First of all, it's a good reminder that, no matter how sophisticated she may seem, her perspective is still that of a child. You and I know that the 1980s were just *yesterday,* but to a ten-year-old they were the Ice Age. The positive message here is that your daughter sees you as the parent, the figure of authority who has standards born in a different time. You probably aren't falling into the trap of trying to be her friend.

If you hear this complaint again and again, however, you may want to give it some thought and discuss it with your daughter. She may be trying to say that she doesn't feel you're relevant, that you don't know enough about her life. In that case, she needs you to engage with her more, to be available more often, to ask more questions, and, above all, to listen more to what she has to say.

What If You Said . . .

If your young upstart calls you old-fashioned, consider these tactics for continuing the conversation.

Confuse her:

Oh, honey, you don't realize that I was already really old in the eighties.

Confuse her some more:

Wait a minute. Did we even have TV in the eighties?

Start a heavy conversation:

You're right, things have changed a lot in the last 20 years, and I don't like all the changes. Not all of them are good for our family.

Move toward the heart of the issue:

Moms and dads always seem old-fashioned to their kids. It's inevitable because you're somebody new with dreams of your own.

Look at it from where she stands, and try to be more 21st-century:

Talk to me about the difference between having a TV in the den and having one in your room. I may not change my mind, but I promise to listen.

"YOU LIED ABOUT WHERE YOU'D BE"

Mom: *Where were you? I called Elise's and you weren't there. You said you'd be there.*

Girl: *I was.*

Mom: *That's not what Elise's mom said.*

Girl: *She was upstairs. We were in the basement.*

Mom: *She checked and you weren't there. You're lying to me.*

Girl: *That's because you never let me do anything. I was at Terri's. She and I walked to the park—no big deal. And it's none of your business!*

What Just Happened?

If your daughter lies to you, she is sending a message of some sort. In the dialogue above, the girl lies in order to do what she feels ready to do. She is telling her mom, "Your rules are too restrictive. I've grown beyond them." At other times, girls lie to us in order to have some privacy. They don't want us to have the power of knowing every little thing about them. Often, I-need-some-privacy lies are lies of omission. They're a girl's way of saying, "Don't be so intrusive. Some parts of my life are my own."

All too often, the lies a girl tells us backfire. A girl wants more trust or privacy from us and so she lies to get it, but when we find out, we trust her less, not more. That's why it's so important for parents to consider carefully and try to translate the messages that lies send.

If you discover your daughter in an occasional lie, do your best not to stage a confrontation. Remember that at least part of what's going on is developmental, as opposed to personal. Nearly every girl lies to her parents about something sometime in the course of developing the "separate" parts of herself. If your daughter develops a pattern of lying to you, address the lack of trust between you. If her safety or well-being is put at risk by her lies, then you must intervene directly. Be clear about the rules and about the consequences for breaking them. But if her lies don't put her at risk, let her know that a certain degree of privacy is appropriate at every age. Assure her that you'll try to give her the room she needs to grow.

What If You Said . . .

If you discover your daughter in a lie, think about the message she may be sending.

I know you need to keep some things to yourself. I understand some things are private, but I need to know when your plans change.

I want to trust you. Help me understand why you just told me something that wasn't true. I'll bet you had a reason.

You didn't want to tell me that you went to the park with Terri. Can you talk to me about why you needed to keep that secret?

My concern is your safety. It's the thing I care about most in this world. Help me figure out how to help you stay safe—whether you're at the park or at Elise's.

I know you can take care of yourself in many situations. That's clear to me—you're very capable. But I worry about you, too. I can't help that, because I'm your parent and I love you. I'll be able to worry less and trust you more if you're honest with me about where you are and with whom.

"BECAUSE I'M THE PARENT, THAT'S WHY!"

Dad: *Hey, what are you doing on the computer again? I thought you'd had your hour and a half today.*

Girl: *Nothing. I'm just talking with some people Chelsea knows.*

Dad: *Wait a minute. You're supposed to chat and instant message only with people you know in real life.*

Girl: *But Dad, these are Chelsea's friends!*

Dad: *Honey, Chelsea is two years older than you are. Do these people all go to her school?*

Girl: *I don't know. But anyway, they all know each other. You can tell.*

Dad: *I want you to sign off. Tell them POS (parent over shoulder) and sign off. I can't let you talk to people online if you don't know their names and faces in real life. They may not be who they say they are.*

Girl: *Dad, no! This is okay. Chelsea's parents let her do it!*

Dad: *I'm not Chelsea's dad. I'm yours. Sign off.*

What Just Happened?

Much of this chapter has been about avoiding verbal shutdowns and conversational dead ends. Overall, your goal as a parent is to keep the conversation going with your daughter. But for all of us, there are points at which we simply have to say no and no and no again. In our busy lives, we don't have all the time we need to explore every situation thoroughly. Besides, girls do tend to push beyond limits that are safe for them. As we've said, that is their job. Because of all those factors, there will be times when you feel you don't know enough or the situation is not safe enough, or you simply intuit in your gut that this situation is riskier than it might appear. You and I have to trust our instincts about what our daughters are ready for. And then we say no.

Think of this as modeling self-trust for your daughter. We want girls to learn to trust their feelings, too. If a girl is walking alone in the parking lot behind her school and things don't seem quite right to her—that is, her unconscious tells her something is amiss in the situation—then we want her to trust that feeling, be on the alert, and leave the area. The same goes for you when you've looked at the situation through her eyes, brainstormed the middle ground, and asked all the right questions, but you *still* don't feel the situation is reasonably safe. You have to say no even if you don't know all the reasons why. At some level, our daughters understand our reasoning when we do this, despite their protests to the contrary.

What If You Said . . .

Try these words when your instincts tell you a situation your daughter wants to be in is not safe.

I can't tell you all the reasons, but too many little things bother me about this. I have to say no.

This isn't something I'm able to give way on. Your being online with people you don't know firsthand is not a situation I feel comfortable about, no matter what Chelsea's parents let her do.

I know this seems perfectly safe to you, but it doesn't strike me that way. I have to pay attention to that feeling when safety is the issue. So this is the rule—no chatting with strangers.

CHAPTER

Relationships of the Heart

*As your daughter moves from childhood
into adolescence, she needs close friends.
It's normal to feel displaced as she
makes room in her heart for others.*

---

*My reaction to Stacey's relationships with her three
closest friends has been a source of tension between us.
I bristle when her voice is cheerier with them than it is
with me and if she shuts her door when they telephone.
I worry that they will be the source of illicit activities or
dangerous ideas that would never have occurred to
Stacey without them. And I panic that they will somehow
replace me as Stacey's primary source of comfort and
advice and as the recipient of her deepest secrets.*

—Jackie, mother of a 14-year-old girl

*One time my daddy told me my boyfriend was ugly.
It really hurt me because I like him. Later, my dad
apologized and said he was just scared of losing
his little girl. I forgave him.*

—Ashleigh, age 14

When our daughters are little, we get to decide who their friends will be. We choose preschool programs and arrange play dates and sleepovers for them. That begins to change when our school-age daughters start choosing friends on their own. Even as they become more independent, we still have plenty of control over how much time they spend with whom. We're mostly aware of their growing attachment to friends during those isolated, poignant moments when we see them together and feel a subtle shift in our daughters' relationship with us.

A bigger adjustment occurs when a girl is 11 or 12 years old. Around this time, doing and liking the same things (the basis of her friendships when she was younger) become less important than talking together, revealing confidences, and sharing feelings. This is when our daughter's emotional involvement and vulnerability with other girls can make us feel like part of an uncomfortable triangle—daughter, friends, and parents—with parents as the odd ones out.

And then there are boys. During these same years, our daughters develop crushes, learn to flirt, and fall into serious "like." What huge changes! We parents used to be the primary occupants of our daughters' hearts (remember when she adored you?), but now it's crowded in there.

*When Monique was getting ready to go to camp for a
month, she said, "I'm going to be gone for a long time, so
this evening I'd like to——" I finished the sentence for her:
"Spend time with your dad and me, right?" She laughed
and so did I, because we both knew she was going to say she
wanted to spend that evening with her friends. I couldn't
keep from feeling a little sad.*

—*Daphne, mother of a 13-year-old girl*

Most of us will feel a similar sadness, maybe even jealousy, as
our daughters grow up. The girls we love are finding roles to play
and people they care about outside the family. Yet, even when we
feel abandoned or displaced, our appropriate place in this process
is usually on the sidelines keeping a watchful eye, offering guidance and support. Our daughters need us; they always will. But
they need friends, too.

*At first I kept yelling at my daughter about this awful friend
she had, but that didn't work. So after a while I changed
my tack. I would say to her, "I know she must be a good kid
because you've chosen her for your friend. You're a good
kid, and so she must be okay, too, even if I can't see that."
After that she talked more honestly with me. That approach
saved us a lot of bitter tears.*

—*Sherry, mother of a 14-year-old girl*

The Age of "I'm So . . ."

Take a road trip sometime with a couple of 12-year-old best friends
in the backseat. Listen for the inordinate number of sentences that
begin with *I'm so . . .* You'll hear "I'm so crazy about *Lord of the*

Rings." "I'm so weird." "I'm so shy." "I'm so . . ." At first blush, you might think these girls are using language in a competitive way, working at one-upmanship. On the contrary, they are speaking the supremely girlish language of connection. With each "I'm so," a girl puts herself out there for examination, revealing herself in order to find out whether she is the same or different, normal or weird, accepted or rejected. She is figuring out who she is by verbally measuring herself against another girl. At this age, the shape of her identity is fluid. So she finds its edges by voicing herself—"I'm so . . ."—and waiting for the response. If her friend gives her reassurance, as in "Oh, so am I," she feels connected and affirmed. An "Oh, yuck!" or "I'd never do that!" will cause her to reconsider (and maybe even change) what she just said.

All this "I" language gets tiresome to us adults, and at one time or another, most of us have responded with something like, "There

---

Infectious Words

The intense connection among girls was illustrated when a mysterious rash affected schoolgirls in various parts of the United States shortly after the terrorist attack on the World Trade Center in 2001. Doctors and psychologists discovered that the rashes were caused by anxiety, but they wondered why nearly all the kids who got the rash were girls.

"Talk" was the answer. Unlike most boys, the girls were talking a lot to their friends about what had happened, revealing their fearfulness and worry to each other. Those feelings were contagious, and so was the psychosomatic rash that went with them.[1]

---

1. Margaret Talbot, "Hysteria Hysteria," *New York Times,* June 2, 2002, section 6, page 42.

are other people in the world, you know!" The reason our response doesn't change a girl's behavior is that she simply has to go through this stage. Furthermore, she has to go through this identity exercise with her *peers* rather than with her parents.

A "Self" Taking Shape

As our daughters begin morphing into their adult selves, they first have to *imagine* who they will become. A girl simply cannot imagine being you and me (we are too powerful and adult), but she *can* imagine being another girl. During adolescence, a girl seeks out other girls like herself, and with hundreds, maybe thousands, of minute comparisons and confidences, each helps the other do the critical work of building identity. This is why there's so much turmoil, betrayal, volatility, and pain in the friendships of girls this age—because friends matter so deeply. When your daughter shares her heart with her friend, she is at risk. Her deepest self (and a very uncertain self at that) is vulnerable.

Much the same thing happens as our daughters become interested in boys. First they imagine themselves as romantic partners, and then they begin exploring the part. They reveal their feelings and information about themselves to the boys they like—a process that leaves them vulnerable.

No wonder we parents bite our nails. A girl in search of herself takes huge emotional risks. Meanwhile, we serve as ballast on our daughters' stormy relational seas, providing steady love and acceptance and playing a role in our daughters' lives that no friend can ever fill.

Using Her Voice

As your daughter grows, you can hear her development as well as see it. A girl who at age 7 shouted confidently from the top of the jungle gym, "I'm the queen of the fairies!" may take a quieter tone at age 12 and speak in a soft sing-song around boys. Vocal quality—including tone, pitch, volume, and intonation—says a lot. Your daughter's voice is the vehicle that carries her message.

As our girls reach the early teen years, their vocal assertiveness often disappears and their strong voices are replaced with high, uncertain tones. These new, wispy voices should signal to us that our daughters feel tentative or nervous about being accepted. We might hear their voices change when they talk on the phone with boys or when they talk to girls who belong to a group outside their own.

We can encourage our daughters to practice speaking forthrightly with their friends and to use a deeper, richer tone. Tape-recording your daughter's voices with her and exploring different ways of speaking—focusing on her natural, deeper voice—can help her retain her authority and communicate self-confidence and self-worth as she navigates the social mazes of growing up.

"SHE'S A BAD INFLUENCE ON YOU"

Girl: *Mom, can Kim come over?*

Mother: *Again? She was just here yesterday. Why don't you invite somebody else?*

Girl: *'Cause I want to invite Kim. You always act like this about her. You don't like her.*

Mother: *This has nothing to do with liking her. She gets into trouble. You know that.*

Girl: *You hate her! She's not bad. You don't know her like I do!*

What Just Happened?

When our daughters choose friends whose standards or goals aren't as high as we'd like, we often say negative or doubtful things about those friends. Unfortunately, our comments cause our daughters to dig in their heels and defend those friends against us. The result can be an impasse.

At points like these, it may help you to remind yourself of this friend's superficial influence as opposed to your deeper influence. Researchers find that girls do conform to peer expectations about superficial matters like clothes and entertainment. **At a more fundamental level, though, our daughters generally hold the same opinions and values as we do on important issues such as moral principles and educational goals.** Meanwhile, however, our daughters feel obligated to defend their friends to us. In fact, when you criticize a friend, your daughter probably feels that you're criticizing her, too, and so she reacts.

It also helps to know how girls influence each other. Research has shown that "bad" girls don't usually say "Hey, try this" to other girls. Rather, the girls who make poor decisions like shoplifting or smoking influence other girls simply by association. Our daughters see other girls doing these things and feel compelled to experiment so that they'll feel connected to their friends, not because of overt pressure. Girls don't want to hurt others' feelings or feel isolated by not joining in. Thus, "bad" behavior often has a lot to do with feelings and with caring for another girl.[2]

You can use this information when you talk with your daughter about friends you'd prefer she stay away from. When we respect and acknowledge our daughters' relationships with other girls—even as we warn them about poor decisions—our words are more likely to be heard.

What If You Said . . .

If you are fearful about a friend's influence on your daughter, be sure to respect their friendship as you talk about good decisions and high standards.

I know you feel close to Kim. I can see that she's a friend. If you like her, there must be some really good things about her that I can't see. Can you tell me more about her?

I can see that Kim is your friend, and I respect that, but I do worry that you might make some of the same decisions she does. I want to talk with you about ways you can be her friend but make different choices.

You ought to be able to choose your own friends. But can you help me trust that your strong character will be a positive force in the friendship? Can you be with Kim and not make the same choices she does?

2. Diane Hales, *Just Like a Woman: How Gender Science Is Redefining What Makes Us Female* (New York: Bantam Books, 1999).

"SHE MUST NOT BE MUCH OF A FRIEND"

Dad: *You're pretty quiet tonight, Jenny. Is something wrong?*

Girl: *It's Sarah. She was talking all day to Adria, and she ignored me. It was awful.*

Dad: *Did you try to talk to her about it?*

Girl: *(with tears in her eyes) Yes, but it didn't help.*

Dad: *Well, she must not be much of a friend if she didn't—*

Girl: *Stop it, Dad! You never understand!*

What Just Happened?

Have you noticed how easy it is to say dismissive things about your daughter's friendships—something like, "Well, there are lots of other girls to be friends with," or "Who needs a friend like that?" Our daughters' friendships appear flighty and undependable—and they are. Almost overnight, a best friend can become an ex-friend. Girls this age can't manage several close friendships at once like adults can, so their friendships are often fragile and full of jealousy. When we parents see all this turmoil, we want to help, so we dismiss these friendships as unimportant. After all, if our daughters could do the same, they'd feel much less pain.

Yet this approach almost never works. Having strong, even passionate, feelings for friends is one way girls grow up and figure out who they are. Our daughters don't have the dispassionate perspective of adults. They are caught in the middle of these torturous friendship changes, and we parents have to acknowledge their feelings in order to help.

This can be especially hard for dads to do, because, unlike moms, they may never have experienced the pain of betrayal in childhood friendships. Boys' and girls' friendships tend to operate differently. Most girls have fewer friends than boys do, and they spend more time with those friends. Within girls' friendships, intimacy is the key, whereas for boys the key is usually activity. Generally speaking, boys play games together in which there are winners and losers, but girls spend time just bonding.

Even the words they use illustrate this difference. Unlike boys, girls don't usually give orders to each other when they're together. They make suggestions, beginning sentences with words such as "Let's," "Why don't we," or "You could." Most of the time, girls connect with friends more than they compete.[3]

What If You Said . . .

When your daughter is rejected by a friend, be sure to acknowledge the pain of displacement when you respond to what she tells you.

Ouch. That must have hurt if she wouldn't talk to you about it.

I know friendships can change fast, but this sounds really hard. I'm sorry you got hurt today.

You are such a good person and a good friend. I'm sorry your feelings are hurt. Do you have a plan for how you might handle this when you go to school tomorrow?

3. Deborah Tannen, *You Just Don't Understand* (New York: Morrow Avon, 1990). Tannen first noticed this tendency in adults and then, curious to see when it started, extended her research to look at school-age kids. She found the children had the same gender-based language differences.

"YOU'RE JEALOUS OF MY FRIENDS"

Girl: *Mom, I want to spend the night at Carrie's.*

Mom: *Again? Why do you want to sleep over there?*

Girl: *So we can watch movies and stuff.*

Mom: *I'd rather you stayed home.*

Girl: *Why do you always say this? It's like you're jealous or something!*

What Just Happened?

As our daughters spend more time with friends, we may feel some jealousy. This happens more often with parents of only children or with first children. When our daughters are young, we parents are the center of their lives; they depend on us for absolutely everything. But our fierce protectiveness and attachment—terrific qualities in a parent of a young child—have to be moderated as our daughters become adolescents so that they can mature and make room in their hearts for others. Faced with that loss, we may say things we later regret. As one mother confessed to me, "When she asks to go see her friends, I don't say no, but I baste my words in a tone of disapproval designed to undermine her pleasure. Then later I feel guilty."

Jealousy can lead to fights in which we find ourselves insisting on our place in our daughters' lives without really analyzing what is at the heart of the matter. **Any time we find ourselves criticizing our daughters' friends, it's a good idea to ask whether or not we feel anxious about being displaced.** This can also be a signal that we need to take more time for ourselves and develop more of our own interests now that our daughters are becoming independent.

Sometimes it may not be jealousy we're feeling but something related—fear. We fear losing the most precious thing in our lives. Of course, at the conscious level, we proclaim loud and clear that our goal in parenting is to prepare our daughters for independence. But with each new phase, that effort takes its toll on our hearts. Even as we prepare our girls to fly, we feel the loss. The psychologist Rachel Billington reminded us of the reason we go through this heartache when she wrote, "A loving and careful mother both recognizes and even protects her daughter's autonomy and helps her dance out confidently onto a wider stage."[4]

What If You Said . . .

If you feel jealous of your daughter's friends, voice the joy it gives you to be with your child, and let her know you respect her need for others in her life.

Maybe you're right. I do miss having you around. I like hearing your laughter around the house. Can you understand that it's not the same around here without you?

Jealousy? Maybe that's the right word, but I'm not sure. I know that I feel a little sad you're growing up fast and will leave home someday and I won't be able to see you as much. I do want to spend more time with you. Can we compromise somehow?

I know you need time with your friends—of course you do. But you and I need time with each other, too. How can we work this out?

4. Rachel Billington, *The Great Umbilical: Mothers and Daughters, the Unbreakable Bond* (London: Hutchison, 1995).

"GET A LIFE, MOM!"

Mom: *(driving the carpool; the girls in the backseat are singing a hit song) Oh, I love that song. That band is so cool.*

Daughter: *(over the noise of the other girls) Mom, nobody says "cool" anymore.*

Mom: *Okay, everybody, tell me the latest! Is that cute Darryl still dating Ellen?*

Daughter: *(beneath her breath) Mom, stop it.*

Various Girls: *They were . . . She was so excited. She told everybody. . . . They broke up at the ball game. Did you hear about that?*

Mom: *They broke up? Really, why?*

Daughter: *Mom, just drive, will you?*

Mom: *I'm just asking what's going on. What's wrong with that?*

Daughter: *You're my <u>mom</u>, that's what. Get a life!*

What Just Happened?

If your daughter has ever snapped at you for being too involved in her social life, you know what a surprise it can be. Of course, you're fond of your daughter's friends. You care about them and enjoy talking with them. But if you get swept away into the excitement of your daughter's social life, that's something altogether different, and your daughter is generally the first person to recognize what's happening.

As adults, we seldom realize how much our own childhoods still affect us, but they do. Our adolescent triumphs and defeats—and the feelings that went with them—lie just beneath the surface of our adult lives. And our daughters have an uncanny knack for zeroing in on those feelings when they surface. Perhaps the mom in our dialogue didn't feel included when she was a girl. That long-ago loneliness may reveal itself in her overzealous interest in her daughter's social set. She takes vicarious pleasure in hearing the new gossip among the girls. To some degree, this is normal. We all feel pleased when our daughters are popular, and we all get energy from the social buzz they bring into our lives. When the boundaries blur between our daughters' social lives and our own, however, conflict is inevitable.

If your daughter tells you, "Get a life," or "They're my friends, not yours," work consciously to pull back from getting into the middle of her social interactions. She needs you there to keep an eye on things, but not to be part of the party. It's truly a gift to her, and to yourself, to recognize her experiences as her own.

What If You Said . . .

If you and your daughter are clashing about your involvement in her social life, think carefully about your past and about old needs that may be surfacing for you. And try these responses:

I understand that you're irritated with me, but when you say, "Get a life!" I feel offended. Try again. Find a respectful way of making that request. Then I'll be more likely to understand your point.

Sorry I got too involved. I can see that I was getting in between you and your friends. They're such fun to talk to that I get carried away. I'll try to remember to back off a little.

At your age, I would've been thrilled to have such good friends. Still, I need to remember that this is your time and these are your friends. If you'll remind me of that respectfully, I'll try to act more like a parent and less like a friend when they're around.

"ANGIE'S GOT A BOYFRIEND . . ."

Girl: *Hi, Dad.*

Dad: *Hi. There's another message on the phone for you from "you know who."*

Girl: *(blushing) Stop it, Dad. You always tease me about Matt.*

Dad: *(in a singsong voice) Angie's got a boyfriend . . .*

Girl: *I mean it! Stop!*

What Just Happened?

Why do we tease our daughters about boys? It's because multiple feelings are at work within us. When our daughters show interest in boys, we're curious about what's going on. Maybe we smile and think the situation is sweet. Maybe we get vicarious pleasure from the fact that our daughter is discovering romance. Also, depending on a girl's age and the boy who is paying attention, we may fear that this is starting when our daughter is too young or that she doesn't need to "go with" anybody yet. Maybe we're afraid we don't know everything that's going on. Maybe we feel nervous because we know these early stages of romance are just the beginning, with more serious attachments ahead. Unable to talk about those feelings straightforwardly, we tease.

And how do our daughters hear this teasing? Sometimes, they perceive the affection. Sometimes girls know that parents, especially dads, are at a loss to talk about budding romances, and so they tease instead. **But more often, girls interpret teasing as our inability to appreciate how serious these first romances are to them, and how keenly they feel the emotions involved.** This is serious work for a girl—learning to perceive herself as a romantic partner, learning to trust someone else with her feelings.

Indeed, as her relationships become more serious, we want to be in the loop. We want her to keep talking. That's why teasing is usually a bad idea. It can cause her to shut us out of this important process.

What If You Said . . .

If you are tempted to tease your daughter about boys, try to identify the feelings that make you want to tease. Most likely, those are feelings that she needs to hear you voice.

Sorry I was teasing. I guess I feel a little nervous about Matt calling all the time.

I'll try not to tease you any more about him. I know that one day you'll grow up and fall in love with somebody and leave home. Thinking about all that makes me sad, because I'll miss you. Sometimes I tease you to cover up those sad feelings.

I shouldn't have teased you. Sorry. I'd also like to talk with you about what's going on with Matt. I know you're "going with" him. What does that mean in sixth grade?

Teasing is a way I try to connect with you. You'll have to let me know when it's not appropriate.

If She Says He's Just a Friend

If your daughter says a particular boy is just a friend, he may very well be just that. Our middle-school daughters are much more likely than we were to be friends with boys. These days, boys are included in girls' friendship circles and cliques. Sometimes girls call these boys "guy friends" or even—and this is confusing— "boy friends." One of my daughters has a friend she refers to as "my girlfriend Jimmie"—meaning that she can really talk to him and he knows how to listen.

"YOU'RE CALLING HIM AGAIN?"

Girl: *(giggling, runs into room and picks up the phone, whispers)*
Okay, when he answers, ask if he likes Kira. Shhh!

Mom: *What are you doing?*

Girl: *(covers mouthpiece) Jana and I are calling Will.*

Mom: *Again? Can't you two do something other than call boys?*

Girl: *Shhh!*

Mom: *Don't shush me. Hang up the phone. I want to talk with
you about this. It gives boys the wrong impression—and their
families, too. Will's parents will think you're an airhead!*

Girl: *Moooommm! Please, no.*

Mom: *Yes. (taking the phone and hanging up)*

Girl: *You have no right to do that!*

What Just Happened?

This mother is coming up against a situation lots of us
encounter. Girls now call boys routinely—whether those
boys are just friends or romantic interests. However, girls often
go through a stage, usually in fifth or sixth grade, when they get
together in giggling groups, call boys, and ask embarrassing
questions—sometimes without telling the boy that a whole group
of girls is listening in.

If your daughter is in the middle of a phone call to a boy, and
you know the call is either inappropriate or simply one call too
many, remember that what she's doing is very common, and you
don't need to make more of it than it is. Preteen girls try to get the
attention of boys they like in awkward ways, and boys who like

particular girls reach out just as awkwardly, mostly by teasing.

It is interesting that girls call mostly when they're together in groups. It might be worth pointing out to your daughter that the girls are more likely to be proving something to each other than to be actually reaching out to a boy. (This may help her understand how unfair such calls can feel to the unsuspecting boy and his family. Calling as a group is a little like bullying.)

We parents are also sensitive to the stereotype these calls support. Whether this mom knows Will's parents or not, she doesn't want other adults thinking of her daughter as boy-crazy or promiscuous. Yet explaining such apprehensions can be tricky, because we don't want to imply that we buy into those stereotypes, either.

What If You Said . . .

When you talk with your daughter about group calls, appeal to her feelings. Mention the boy's probable embarrassment and the impression such calls leave with his family.

I'm sorry I used the word "airhead." I had a strong reaction to seeing you call Will again. I don't think you mean any harm, but let's talk about how it appears to Will's parents if you call him again and again. What are they experiencing? Then let's discuss some ground rules for calls when you have friends over.

Let's talk about Will. Have you thought about how he feels if you ask him personal questions? Would you feel okay about asking him the same things in person?

You know, these conference calls seem unfair to me—as if you're ganging up on one person. Is there anything unkind in what you're doing? What if Will doesn't know who else is listening when he talks about Kira?

"YOU LOOK LIKE A TRAMP"

Girl: *Mom, we're going to Rick's house to watch a movie. I'm going to walk over and meet Rachel now.*

Mom: *Who is "we"? And what movie will you be watching?*

Girl: *Rachel and John, and Rick and me. I'm not sure about the movie. Rick has it already.*

Mom: *Wait a minute. That sounds like two couples and not much supervision.*

Girl: *Well, it's a date, Mom. How much supervision is there supposed to be on a date? (as she walks out the door)*

Mom: *Stop! I need to know more. Will Rick's parents be there? Never mind—you're not going anyway. Look at the way you're dressed! You're starting to look and act like a tramp!*

What Just Happened?

If our daughters hear words like *tramp, slut,* or *whore* from us, they never forget it. If you find yourself having said these words, make amends as quickly as you can. If you need to, ask a friend or a counselor to help you and your daughter talk about what happened and how you can clear the air.

Meanwhile, identify the feelings that lie behind such strong accusations. Fear is always part of the mix when a parent calls a girl names like these. Maybe you're afraid your daughter is adrift and at risk. Maybe you fear she doesn't understand the powerful impact sexual activity can have on her. (Your fears are well grounded. Most girls don't.) Maybe you fear she is losing touch with you as she becomes more involved with boys.

Anger plays a role, too. Accusations are usually a signal that something got away from us. Maybe you weren't watching closely enough and she moved into a different, more serious phase of a relationship with a boy. Maybe you're angry because you didn't talk with her sooner, thinking she had a few years more before she needed your guidance about sex. It's natural for you to feel betrayed or blindsided by these developments.

But name-calling never works. It only destroys trust, drives girls away, and sometimes even gives them license to act in the way we've accused them of acting. No matter what the situation, find a friend or counselor to help you process your own feelings. Then apologize to your daughter and talk with her about what's going on. This is a powerful model of love for your daughter. Since we all make mistakes and have to start over now and then, this is an opportunity for you to show her how.

What If You Said . . .

If you accused your daughter of sexual activity and spoke harshly to her, think carefully about how you'll rebuild trust and respect.

I was wrong to say that about you. It's not true, and I am sorry. Even if I was really angry, I shouldn't have insulted you. Can we talk calmly about your plans for tonight?

I wish I hadn't said that. Please forgive me for treating you so disrespectfully, but I'm really afraid for you sometimes. There's so much risk in sexual activity, and I don't think we've talked enough about that.

I'm not sure I knew that you'd moved to this kind of dating, and it upset me. But still, I should never have talked to you like that. I'm sorry I lost my temper. Can we start that conversation over?

CHAPTER

Close Quarters

*Sometimes just living together
in the same house is hard work.*

---

*I often hear myself asking "why?" I say, "Why don't you
hang your towels up? Why do you leave things on the
stairs? Why do you leave your dishes in the den?"
And I don't like my voice when I say that. There's a
judgment in it, like, "What's wrong with you, kid?"*

—Janie, mother of girls ages 10 and 13

*One morning we all woke up on the wrong side of the
bed. My brother threw a temper tantrum, and I started
crying, too. It made my mom stressed, and out of her
anger she said, "Where do these children come from?"
She didn't know I had heard her, and I was
too hurt to say anything.*

—Kasey, age 11

Ironically, the very things that make us families—sharing space and sharing time—also challenge us on a day-to-day basis. The mechanics of keeping a household running are stressful to begin with, and as girls grow up, evolving into creatures with wills and schedules of their own, friction is inevitable. Girls and parents in nearly every family we talked with reported conflict and regretted words around two subjects—sleep and chores. In these areas, negotiations, agreements, and temporary truces appear to be the ongoing norm. In fact, when we parents joke about shipping daughters off until they're 21, we're usually frustrated about some little thing—some undone chore or a petty but troublesome demand on our time—that adds to the stress of living in close quarters.

Mornings—the Big-Time Time Crunch

When are you most likely to exchange harsh words with your daughter? For most of us, the answer is "in the morning." We parents see girls at their most vulnerable and most difficult because we are the ones who have to rouse them from sleep, put them on their feet, and send them out to meet the day. Generally speaking, the adolescent brain does not wake quickly, and during the period when a girl transitions between sleep and wakefulness, she is stressed and overreactive—weepy or angry, depending on the girl. Girls simply cannot cope with frustration early in the morning the way they can cope later in the day. The 13-year-old who seems so self-pitying in this story may be confident at noon, but not at 6 A.M.

> *Last week I woke up on a school morning exhausted. My throat was scratchy and my eyes stung when I put my contacts in. My parents said I should have gone to bed on time so I wouldn't have been tired and I could have dealt better with my other problems. I started crying, and my dad told me to explain what was wrong. I tried, but my voice was hoarse. He yelled at me for not talking so that he could understand me.*
>
> *—Julianne, age 13*

This kind of helplessness is frustrating to deal with, especially when we have a household to run and a day of work ahead of us. Like this girl's parents, you might tell your daughter to go to bed earlier, but that may not solve the problem. Puberty shifts a girl's sleep pattern. Her brain and body want to go to bed later and sleep later the next morning. The "natural" hour for our adolescent daughters to wake up is more like 9 A.M. than 6 A.M. Research shows that adolescents who start the school day later are more alert in class, make better grades, and feel better about themselves. But most girls don't have that option, so they run chronically short on sleep. One study of 12- and 13-year-olds found that half of them could enter a sleeplike state in only three or four minutes *in the middle of the day.* Their sleep debt was so large that their brains were actually more asleep than awake.[1]

Clearly, first thing in the morning, you and I are more or less

1. Dr. Mary Carskadon, Brown University, discussing her 1999 research on 6,000 middle-school students, in a conversation with A. Lynch, January 2001.

dealing with sleepwalkers. We have to adjust our words and expectations accordingly.

Doing Chores

The end of the day presents different problems. With the deadline
of bedtime in front of us, we parents rush to get everything done
and to get the household to bed at a reasonable hour. When we're
tired, we're most aware of our need for help with the work of main-
taining the household and most likely to be angry about the chores
our daughters leave undone.

If your household is typical, the parents do 90 percent of the
housework. That's right. You do *nine* chores for every *one* your
daughter does. And if your household is like mine, it's an excep-
tional day when your daughter helps out without complaining or
being reminded several times first. This kind of frustration can
lead us to say hurtful things.

> *Once my mom asked me to do some cleaning and I forgot.*
> *I was watching TV in the living room when my mom came*
> *in. We were having guests over, so she asked if I'd done my*
> *chores. I admitted that I hadn't, and she said in a voice*
> *that made me feel horrible, "You're useless!"*
>
> —*Allie, age 10*

Of course we feel for Allie—no kid should be told she's useless
by her parent. But no parent should have to do all the chores herself either.

You may remember doing lots of daily chores around the
house as a kid, but these days family life is different. With both parents working and higher academic standards for our daughters,

everybody is stressed and busy. Our daughters don't have as much time to do chores as you and I did when we were kids, and you and I don't have the time our parents did to follow through and supervise. Inevitably, we have words.

I don't know how many times I've been through this with my daughter. We decide on a chore that Cara agrees to do every week. She seems willing, and at first it works out okay, but then after a while she starts to forget and it doesn't get done. I remind her a few times, but then one day I just get tired and blow up at her. Then she cries and I feel bad and we start all over again.

—Paolo, father of a 13-year-old girl

The good news in Paolo's story may be in the final words—"we start all over again." Part of what's happening when parents and daughters clash over chores is a normal learning process. Girls don't grow up and become responsible overnight. Responsibility is a lesson we have to teach over and over before they learn it. Failings on their part, and on ours, are part of the process.

Time helps, too. The 12-year-old who can't be bothered with taking out the trash will amaze you at age 14 by cleaning the kitchen without being asked. Girls do take on more responsibility, but slowly. In time, they learn to consider the needs of the whole household. Meanwhile, we parents learn the fine art of distinguishing between the issues that we need to make a big deal about—because, like submariners, we and our daughters are on this vessel together—and those issues that we can be patient about for the sake of a peaceful voyage.

"WAKE UP—NOW!"

Dad: *(knocking on his daughter's door) Let's go. Time to get up.*

Dad: *(five minutes later, knocking loudly) Kelly, did you hear me? Come on, move it or you're going to be late!*

Dad: *(ten minutes later, barging into her room, flipping on the light) I can't believe you're still in bed. You'll make everybody late! Get up NOW!*

What Just Happened?

The dad in this scenario is doing what most of us do to wake our daughters. Unfortunately, as his frustration builds, he chooses words that can only cause friction. This is one of those times when what we say is not necessarily what our daughters hear. When this dad says, "Come on, move it," his half-awake daughter is in such a vulnerable state that she is likely to hear, "What's wrong with you?" When he says, "You'll make everybody else late," she hears, "You're a loser. You never do anything right." Next thing you know, she gets up and yells at him, and the day is off to a terrible start.

When we wake our daughters, we do well to say something encouraging and loving. Use your daughter's name—that helps pull her from groggy sleep to her daytime self—and look for words that can't be easily interpreted as criticism. "Hey, time to conquer the world again" might be a good choice (especially if it makes her laugh), or simply "Good morning, sweetie. It's going to be a good day."

A hug and a nuzzle can help, too, though your daughter may be especially sensitive to touch at this time. A good friend of mine remembers her dad's well-intentioned efforts to wake her with back rubs in the morning—but they hurt because she wasn't ready to have her shoulders scrunched at that early hour. Whether you're talking or touching, be gentle this time of day. Whatever you do is likely to feel exaggerated to your daughter as she struggles to wake, and it sets the tone for your interactions all day long.

What If You Said . . .

When you wake your daughter, remember how difficult it is for her to transition to being awake.

Good morning, honey. Did you have good dreams? I put the funnies on the kitchen table, so you can read them while you eat.

Good morning, Kelly. I love you. There's a new day out there waiting for you.

How's the girl I love this morning? Rise and shine, Kelly.

If (when) this doesn't work, your next step is to talk about time.
It's 6:30, honey. Your breakfast will be on the table in five minutes.

"YOU'RE LATE ALREADY!"

Mom: *(knocking on bathroom door) What are you doing in there? You're going to be late!*

Girl: *(no answer)*

Mom: *Did you hear me? Answer me! It's time to go!*

Girl: *(opening door) Stop it! You're driving me crazy. I can't go looking like this! My hair is terrible! Just look at it!*

Mom: *Your hair is the least of my worries right now. We've got to leave now or we're not going to make it.*

Girl: *You don't even care about me!*

What Just Happened?

If you are a 10- or 12-year-old girl, it can be excruciatingly difficult to get dressed and fix your hair in the morning. Not only do you have to morph from your private self (the one who was blissfully asleep) to your public self (the one who has to go to school), but you know that once you're at school, the other girls will evaluate (and none too kindly) how well you pulled off this transition. If you can't achieve the look you're trying for, the morning is more or less ruined. Furthermore, most fifth- and sixth-graders are not very skilled at getting the look they want, so they put in lots of time and *still* feel frustrated.

You and I can't really change this dynamic, but we can avoid getting hooked into our daughters' frustration. **If your daughter is running late, try to offer comments about time management rather than about the girl herself.** Finally, consider the advice about consequences from the following mother. It's a way of backing out of the morning "You're going to be late!" loop.

*Mornings were when I used to always yell at her, "We're
going to be late! We're going to be late!" Finally I got tired
of that and gave myself a choice—either keep yelling, or
state my expectations and let it be. Now, the night before,
I say, "If you're up by 7:15, you won't be late for school." Or
that morning I say, "You have ten minutes to get dressed
in order to be on time." Then, if she's late, she's late, and
I don't take that on as my problem. She has to take the
consequences. I won't make excuses for her or write a note.
You wouldn't believe how much that has helped.*

—Theodorah, mother of a 13-year-old girl

What If You Said . . .

When she's running late and all seems lost, acknowledge
how hard it is for her to pull herself together at this age, and
offer your comments in terms of time management.

*I'm sorry your hair isn't doing exactly what you wanted. We have
five minutes. Can I help?*

*I can see you're really upset about this. I'm sorry your hair is
frustrating you this morning. We have 15 minutes in the car.
Why don't you grab a mirror and use those minutes to get
your hair in line?*

*This is a difficult time of day for all of us, and right now we're out
of time. I have to pull out of the driveway at 6:40—that's in
three minutes—so that I won't be late for a meeting. You have
a choice. Either brush your hair back and come on, or catch a
ride with your dad, in which case you'll have to explain your
tardiness to your teacher.*

"YOU ARE SO LAZY!"

Mom: *Lilly, you didn't unload the dishwasher.*

Girl: *You didn't ask me to.*

Mom: *That's your job; you know that. You don't have to be asked every time!*

Girl: *Fine!*

Mom: *We __all__ have work to do around here, missy. You are so lazy!*

What Just Happened?

The parents and girls interviewed for this book reported saying and hearing the words "lazy," "ungrateful," and "spoiled" when it came to housework. In general, the parents reported feeling resentment because their daughters didn't do enough. Meanwhile, the girls reported resentment, too—for being asked to do *so much.* Their perception and ours are worlds apart! No wonder we clash when it's time to take out the trash or fold the clothes.

The mom in the scenario above may be tempted to give up. It takes all of five minutes to unload the dishwasher, so why not do it herself and be done with it? Yet, we do our daughters no favors when we protect them from responsibility or assume that their contribution to the family doesn't matter. In fact, you and I have to instill a sense of contribution and generosity in the girls we love if they are to grow up feeling a sense of achievement and purpose.

It may help the mom in the scene above to think in terms of *rewriting the story.* Right now, the story she's spinning is that her daughter is lazy. She could try a "rewrite" that assumes her daughter is responsible. She could say something like, "I know there's a lot of pressure on you. All of us are busy. That's why the contribution you make around here is so important." This gives the girl a chance to make good on those terms. We parents can also reframe the story a bit by using the word "contribution" instead of "chore." Nobody likes to do chores, but we all feel valued if we contribute.

Finally, you can remember that your daughter will mature eventually and become more aware of the needs of people around her. Reframing the situation in these ways won't make a magical difference overnight—responsibility is an ongoing lesson we have to teach—but it may help you avoid a showdown in the immediate moment, when regrettable words have been said.

What If You Said . . .

When you clash over chores, try these approaches to clearing the air and steering the conversation toward positive ideas.

I'm sorry I called you lazy. I get really tense about keeping the housework under control. When you unload the dishwasher, it may seem like a boring, pointless thing, but it makes a really big difference to me.

I know you aren't lazy. In fact, there are lots of things you're very responsible about. I really need you to unload the dishwasher each day, and it makes me feel good knowing that most of the time I can depend on you to do it. Your contribution around here matters.

Being flexible about the time frame, but not the task, may allow her to save face and allow you to get her cooperation.

I do need to have the dishes put away. Let's say you do that by seven. Then I can do the dinner dishes after that.

"STOP NAGGING ME!"

Mom: *Rochelle, your backpack is still in the middle of the living room floor. I told you to pick it up.*

Girl: *(no answer)*

Mom: *Did you hear me? I've asked you three times now.*

Girl: *Don't I know it!*

Mom: *What kind of tone is that?*

Girl: *It's the tone you get when you nag me all the time!*

What Just Happened?

No kid wants to hear us remind her again and again about chores that she needs to do. None of us wants to nag. But girls *will* ignore or delay helping out around the house, and we parents will get frustrated. Fortunately, when you find yourself in the nagging mode, there are steps you can take. First, reiterate the "why" behind your asking—because your daughter's contribution matters. Next, affirm your belief that she is becoming a responsible person. Believe it or not, she hears that message, and your words do have predictive power.

Finally, look for ways to remind your daughter of undone tasks without sounding like a broken record. You might try leaving humorous e-mails or phone messages for her. ("Hi, I'm the dishwasher, and I'm lonely without you!") Of course, be matter-of-fact about the consequences of leaving work undone. If there is a privilege tied to the task, then the privilege disappears, no questions asked and no nagging attached. And if your disappointment is the only consequence, then you get to voice that, too (but only once, so as not to bore yourself with nagging).

What If You Said . . .

If you find yourself nagging your daughter about chores that have not been done, one of these responses may help:

It must be annoying to hear me telling you to do this all the time. I don't want to nag either, but I do need to know you'll do this task. The help you give around here matters a lot. How can you show me you'll be responsible?

Are there ways I can remind you about this without nagging?

You're right. I'm nagging, and that's a waste of time for both of us. I won't remind you again. You're responsible enough to do it on your own. And if it's not done, you know the consequences.

Maybe we should brainstorm ways to help you organize so that you can get this done. What would help you find time for this task?

You're right. We both want the nagging to stop. Let's talk about a reasonable consequence for not getting your work done. Then I won't have to nag; the consequence will just kick in instead.

I'm disappointed you haven't picked up your things yet. Your cooperation and help mean a lot to me. I won't nag you any more, but I do need you to be aware of my disappointment. I expect more than this from you.

"I SAID GO TO BED!"

Dad: *(starting from his sleep)* What's that noise?

Mom: *(reading in bed)* Nothing, honey. It's Sandra. She's still up.

Dad: But it's nearly midnight. She's supposed to be in bed. *(raising his voice and calling)* Sandra! Go to bed!

Girl: *(calling back)* I tried, but I'm not sleepy. I got up to watch TV.

Dad: I don't care if you can't sleep! I said go to bed!

Girl: But I'm not doing anything wrong! You have no right to yell at me if I'm not doing anything wrong!

Mom: Great! With you two yelling, nobody can sleep!

What Just Happened?

When our daughters are 8 or 10 years old, we put them to bed at a reasonable hour, and that is (more or less) that. Even at 12, most girls go to bed when we decide it's time. But girls of 13 and 14 have a slightly different biology. Maturity shifts their sleep patterns, and they often feel wide awake until late at night. As a result, they tend to be vulnerable and irritable in the morning.

Meanwhile, the opposite happens for us adults, who, unless we're night owls, get tired and cranky late at night. If there's an hour when our daughters seem most unresponsive and unreasonable to us, it's probably 6 A.M. But at midnight, we parents usually win the who-can-be-most-short-tempered contest. Our bodies and our daughters' bodies are in different stages of life and, generally speaking, on very different sleep schedules.

This issue needs negotiation if we're to avoid hurtful words during the wee hours. Find a time when everybody is fully awake—noon, maybe—and have a family meeting about your needs and your daughter's. In the big picture, this is a standard parental passage, running up against the fact that our daughters aren't as pliant as they used to be and that it takes a new level of diplomacy—on their part and on ours—to work out everyday living arrangements. In the end, this process moves our daughters along to young adulthood, and it moves us along, too. One day we wake and find ourselves the parents of teens rather than of little girls.

What If You Said . . .

If her late-night activities are a problem, let her know that you understand her need for a new schedule, but tell her that she has to understand and respect your needs, too. Remember that she's not staying up late just to irritate you—it just feels that way when you're tired.

I realize I've been yelling at you late at night, and I'm sorry if I've hurt your feelings. But we have to have some rules about what you do when you stay up, and just how late you do those things.

Sometimes living together is hard. You're cranky in the morning, and I'm cranky at night. If I can be considerate of you in the morning, then I expect you to be considerate of me and my need for sleep late at night. How can we compromise on this?

I know you're growing up and that staying up late makes you feel independent, but I'm not totally comfortable with your being up while I'm asleep. Can you help me worry less about that? Let's brainstorm some ground rules for when you stay up late.

It doesn't work for you to be up late making noise when I'm tired and need to sleep. That's not even considering your need for more sleep. Let's talk about different rules for weekends and school nights. Maybe that will let us both get what we need.

When Families Change

*Divorce, death of a loved one, moving,
financial loss—big changes bring strong feelings
to the fore. How can you find words that heal
when the whole family is under stress?*

---

*My dad got remarried when I was four. I have always
called my stepmother "Mom." Well, one day, I was really
mad at her and told her that I wished she'd never
married my dad and that we'd be better off without her.
Right after I said it, I wished I hadn't. She cried for
hours, and I had to tell my dad what I had said at dinner.*

—Daisy, age 12

*When my mother died, I didn't realize how deeply
Marie was grieving. She became withdrawn, and so did
I as I pulled back into my own grief. About a month later,
Marie started acting out—getting into a fight at school
and letting her grades drop—and I realized what was
happening. I told her I was sorry I hadn't been there for
her. We had a rough time for a while.*

—Nancy, mother of a 12-year-old girl

Changes in the family—even good changes—are stressful. Uncertainty, grief, and anger accompany any major transition, and those emotions can cause all of us to say words we regret later. Nearly every family has gone through some sort of passage when nothing seemed normal, patience was short, and loving words were hard to find.

Mirrors for Our Emotions

A very young girl can be shielded from lots of events, but a preteen has a broader emotional range. At some level, she's going to feel and express all the emotions the adults in the household are feeling as things change.

Girls and boys are affected by family distress in different ways. Boys tend to feel depressed when the family goes through difficult changes, mostly because their parents have less time to give them. This is true for girls, too, but in addition, girls tend to be *emotionally reactive:* they incorporate our feelings into their own moods. Just as we discussed in chapter 1, "Girls and Words," the girls in our lives usually have sensitive emotional radar systems. They pick up on what we're feeling, intensify the signal, and beam it back to us.

Why She Tests You

This is not to say that girls always react emotionally to changes right away. Sometimes they put their own concerns on the back burner for a while and chip in to help the family get through this tight spot. At other times (usually after the situation has gone on for some time), girls begin to test us either verbally or by acting out. For example, a girl whose parent has cancer has to let off steam somewhere about what's going on. Her other parent is usually the person she feels safest venting to. A girl whose parents have separated may need to talk (or yell) about the abandonment she feels.

Sometimes our daughters just need to test us in order to reassure themselves that, even though things have changed, we're still there for them. In a way, **a girl who challenges or insults you about the family situation is asking, "Just how bad is it, really?"** You are her barometer. If she attacks and you fall apart, then she knows things are bad. But if, when your daughter says the worst, you respond more or less reasonably, she knows you're still her anchor in the storm. She can look to you to steady herself.

Overcoming the "Shoulds"

All new situations come with a set of "shoulds" and "ought tos," and they can bedevil our conversations with our daughters. Does any of this sound familiar? "You shouldn't feel bad about moving, because Mom (or Dad) is happy about this new job." "We should be strong even though Grandpa died." "You should accept your new stepdad."

Focusing on "shoulds" like these can cut us off from our daughters and what they're really feeling. Of course, we can express our hopes for our own behavior and for theirs (this helps us remember that this hard time will pass). But in the meantime it's essential to recognize the changes a girl is experiencing and her immediate feelings about them.

Instead of telling her how she *should* feel, be sure to acknowledge her position and her pain. The bottom line is she has a right to have her own feelings. Otherwise, those feelings are certain to erupt at some other time in words we'll wish we'd never said or heard.

Words That Build Resilience

In How to Mother a Successful Daughter *(New York: Harmony Books, 1999), Nicky Marone advises us to teach our daughters to say three things to themselves when the going is tough. Simplified, they are:*

This is temporary. All things change.

This problem is limited. It's not my whole life.

What's happening is not necessarily my fault. Lots of things in the world are beyond my control.

Use these affirmations for yourself, and teach your daughter to use them, too. A resilient attitude will help both of you find positive words when times are hard or resources are limited.

In Her Own Way

Adjusting to a major change is a lot like getting through grief. Even positive changes produce some grief, because we leave something behind that once served or suited us, but no longer does. Your daughter may be thrilled that moving to a new home means she finally has her own bedroom, but she may still grieve the loss of her old neighborhood and the security of her old home. She may be comforted that having a stepmother around means she's alone less, but she may need to grieve the loss of one-on-one time with her father. Fortunately, the outcome of the grieving process is positive in the end. Grieving leads us to a new place where we can make peace with whatever is gone.

Each of us goes through this process at her own pace and in her own way. You may work through a separation, a financial setback, or a death in the family with occasional outbursts of emotion followed by periods of determination and one-day-at-a-time hard work. Meanwhile, your daughter may appear lost, hyperactive, or disorganized. Grief can look like anger, frustration, confusion, sadness, or acting out.

The girl who's trying to adjust to changed family circumstances may feel compelled to take risks. She may find that she needs to kick a soccer ball every evening until she is exhausted. She may need to weep and write poetry. She may become clingy or distant. No matter what form her reaction takes, your job and mine is to honor her grief process and to support her as she finds her way through it.

Taking Care of Yourself

Likewise, we parents work through transitions in our own ways. This is when a network of support (friends, counselors, your mom, a religious practice, vacation time, and other forms of self-nurturance) is absolutely essential. If we find ways to release some of the pain and pressure we feel, then we're less likely to be ambushed by our own pent-up feelings when we respond to things our daughters do or say. And we're less likely to burden our adolescent daughters with our adult-size problems.

In fact, during any time of radical change in the family, the thing that will give you the most control over your words is not willpower or good intentions. It's not even (though I hate to admit it) reading this book. It is basic self-care—taking the time you need for yourself, caring for your body, and reaching out for support whenever you need it. It's knowing that when the going got tough, you did your best, and it's also forgiving yourself for the times you think you failed. If you take care of yourself so that you can remain strong and centered, you'll be more likely to find the words you and your daughter need to hear. And you'll have the energy to play all of the roles you need to play as the family changes—parent, protector, caregiver, breadwinner, cheerleader, strategist, mourner, crew chief, and, most important, dreamer. As the parent, you are the person who envisions the next stage, the one that comes after this time of change.

"THE DIVORCE IS ALL YOUR FAULT!"

Girl: *Why do I always have to feed the dog? That was Dad's job.*

Mom: *Well, we live here together and we each need to do our part. It doesn't matter if it was Dad's job. It's just something that needs to be done every day.*

Girl: *It does too matter! If you had been nicer to Dad, he would still love you and we wouldn't have to live like this! The divorce is all your fault!*

Mom: *You can blame me for all your problems, but it won't do any good. You and your dad both do that. And blaming the mother—that's the oldest line in the book! Now feed the dog!*

Girl: *This is why Daddy left—because you are such a bitch! Get out of my life!*

What Just Happened?

If you are going through a divorce or separation, you're probably doing your best to keep marital conflict out of earshot of your daughter. Even so, girls usually have a keen sense of family dynamics, and if nothing else, they imagine the conflict you and your spouse are going through. Harsh words from your daughter can be like a punch in the stomach at this time, echoing the rejection of the split. Remember that there's never anything wrong with walking away from words that hurt too much. It's better to take a break than to lash out in response or to let your daughter berate you.

So often when a marriage is dissolving, words over ordinary issues turn acrid. Everybody's stressed, so don't be surprised if this is when your daughter chooses to hit below the belt. Blame is on everybody's mind. A separation or divorce creates a painful sense of dislocation for your daughter. A girl is literally displaced when she has to move, change schools, or start sharing a bedroom with a sibling. Psychologically, her security is gone, too. When the very ground under her feet shifts, she is likely to blame a parent. Needless to say, her words find a ready target. What divorced parent hasn't felt guilty for failing at the marriage he or she tried to build?

The mom in this scenario has reason to be hurt. She's trying to protect her daughter from as much harm as possible, and yet the daughter is on the attack. The mom can do her best not to react to the blaming "bait" her daughter has thrown at her, and she can remind herself (and her daughter) that she's doing her best. Somehow, in the end, that will be enough.

What If You Said . . .

Remember that each time you refuse to fight over who's to blame, your daughter becomes less likely to bring it up again.

Honey, I wish I could make it okay. We all want to blame somebody right now for how awful we feel. I wish you didn't have to do so many chores, too. But I can't change the past, and blaming each other just hurts everybody more. I know this is hard, but if you can be strong right now, the future will be better.

I'm sorry I said that you blame me for everything. This is a hard time for both of us. I mean, feeding the dog is such a little thing, but it feels big when we're both so stressed. Things are hard for you, I know that, but we'll make it if we both do our part.

Okay, let's feed the dog together. Then I want to talk about these feelings. This separation is so complicated, and blaming each other doesn't really help. I love you so much, and that won't change, no matter how hard things are for us.

"YOU'RE JUST MY STEPMOM. YOU DON'T EVEN BELONG HERE"

Stepmother: *Jamie, you aren't allowed to wear that much makeup to school. Your dad has talked with you about this.*

Girl: *Shut up! You can't tell me how much makeup to wear. You're just my stepmom. You don't even belong here.*

Stepmother: *That hurts! All I'm doing is reminding you of the rules. What would your dad think about your talking to me this way?*

Girl: *My dad—ha! He gave up caring about me when you got married. Just leave me alone. You're always trying to turn him against me.*

Stepmother: *That's enough! It's about time you grew up. Your dad is my husband now! (The talk ends with sobbing on both sides.)*

What Just Happened?

Step-relationships come with built-in resentments, but step-mothers and stepdaughters have a particularly difficult time of it. The relationship that gives you and a girl's dad so much joy may bring a feeling of loss and abandonment to your stepdaughter, a sense that the attention she used to get from her dad has been visibly transferred to you. Stepdaughters almost always feel a loss of status when their dads (or their moms) remarry. With a stepparent in the house, a girl falls from a near-peer relationship with her parent back to the former role of child. This is why girls are so often armed for bear when they argue with stepparents. But that doesn't make it okay for them to attack us, or for us to attack back.

Use a light touch with your stepdaughter. Don't rush into the relationship expecting her to see you as an equal co-parent with her father. Ultimately your best role is that of a responsible caretaker who is upholding the rules of the house, which you and your spouse have conveniently agreed upon beforehand, and which take into account the need for your stepdaughter to show you respect. Girls need lots of time to adjust to having stepparents in their lives, and they tend to respond better when we stand back a bit and let them come to us. Be sure not to try to force affection from a stepdaughter (though, in time, very close relationships often develop). Instead, when confrontations arise, calm the storm by focusing on how things work in the household and who is responsible for what.

What If You Said . . .

Try to focus on how decisions are made, rather than on your stepdaughter's feelings about having you as part of the family.

I'm sorry I blew up at you. I don't want to fight with you. I think I'm not entirely clear yet about when to let you make your own decisions. Let's set up a time to talk about this with your dad.

Let's stop. We both crossed the line, and I'm sorry we did. Your feelings about this are obviously very strong.

I'm sorry about what I said. Our relationship is hard because— you're right—I'm not your mom. Yet I am the adult who is around and responsible for you sometimes. I think we both have to cut each other some slack.

This is hard. Our feelings are getting in the way of working this out. Why don't you write down what you think are reasonable rules for your makeup, and we'll have your dad do the same. Then we can make an agreement together. That way I'll know what the rules are when he's gone and I have to take you to school.

"I HATE IT HERE. I WANT TO GO BACK HOME"

Girl: *I'm bored. I don't have anything to do.*

Mom: *Why don't you try calling some of the kids you met at youth group? I'll drive you to a movie if any of them are free to go.*

Girl: *(shrugging) They're all busy.*

Mom: *And you know that how? You haven't tried. You're just feeling sorry for yourself.*

Girl: *You don't know if I've tried or not! You're busy all the time in your big, new super-duper job.*

Mom: *So what if I love my job? That's to your advantage. It pays the bills, doesn't it?*

Girl: *All I know is that I didn't want to move in the first place. I don't have any friends, and it's all your fault. I hate it here! I want to go back home.*

What Just Happened?

In our mobile society, we sometimes forget how important roots are to us. The past grounds us—even the short version of the past that our daughters can remember. If we move, the family temporarily loses its sense of history. For a while, we're bound to feel insecure, and insecure people tend to use harsh words with one another.

It's easy for us parents to focus on the good things about moving, but we also need to talk about our losses. Rituals will help your whole family find words for your experiences and will help you just let pain be pain during the adjustment period. One ritual might include setting aside a special time when the family can talk (or yell or cry) about what has changed. You might create a "memory corner," where photos and relics of your old life are displayed. Create new rituals that allow you to have time with your daughter. Try a regular evening walk, or take outings when you explore a new shop or coffeehouse. These things can help a girl grow roots in a new place—and keep you talking on a regular basis.

Be sure to continue any religious practices that the family had before the move. There's a reassuring sameness among religious communities. Notice those traditions that haven't changed—the way you celebrate holidays, the sports you play together, even the TV shows you enjoy sharing—and make a big deal out of them. They represent continuity at a time when other things feel broken.

What If You Said . . .

If your daughter blames you for her unhappiness in a new place, honor the sense of dislocation she feels.

I can hear what you're saying. Sometimes I wish we could go back to our old place, too. I miss it. What do you miss most?

I'm sorry you blame me. I hope you won't always feel that way. I wish I had complete control over what happens to our family, but I don't. I just control one thing—my feelings for you, which haven't changed. I'll always love you. The setting has changed, but our crazy old family is still the same.

I'm so sorry this is a hard time for you, honey. You're right. I do love my new job, but I never wanted to see you feeling so blue. Blame me if it makes you feel better, but I want to talk about that some-time soon. I'm not sure that blaming anybody does us any good.

I'm so sorry you miss your friends. I know you've been e-mailing, but let's arrange a visit back there for you. That will be something to look forward to.

"YOU NEVER USED TO ACT LIKE THIS"

Dad: *Stacey, for the last time—pick up your room. Your grand-mother will be here any minute.*

Girl: *So? Just shut the door.*

Dad: *What kind of attitude is that? You never used to act like this.*

Girl: *Maybe it's the attitude you deserve from me right now.*

Dad: *So your lousy attitude is my fault? I don't think so. Now pick up your room. Your grandmother and I have to meet about Granddad's estate. I don't want her to see this mess.*

Girl: *THEN SHUT THE DOOR! (slams it herself)*

What Just Happened?

Grief keeps no timetable, and nobody can say when a girl will be able to let go of her grief. The girl whose grandfather dies in October may be sad at Christmas and basically over her grief in the spring. Or if she doesn't find words or healthy ways to express her loss, she is likely to grieve through her behavior. Months after you think she has absorbed the loss, she may become sullen or withdrawn. Maybe she'll push the limits when it comes to sexual behavior or risky activities such as smoking.

Grief can be especially intense and complicated for a girl entering adolescence. She is in the process of figuring out right and wrong, justice and fairness—yet nothing about her suffering feels fair. Just when she's trying to figure out what life means, loss can undermine her sense of purpose or optimism. Finally, a girl who is leaving childhood behind feels that loss, too, and it can make her grief over other changes even more intense. Life may feel chaotic or unreal to her for a while. "Bad" behaviors may be her way of exerting some sort of control over her life.

These sorts of changes in a girl's behavior are not easy for us parents to be patient with, especially since we're grieving our own losses at the same time. Be sure to get professional support for your daughter if she needs it, and ask her teachers, your pastor or rabbi, and other adults in her life to support her as well. Also let your daughter know that you'll listen when she wants to talk about how she's feeling, and that her feelings (all of them) are acceptable, even when her behavior is not.

What If You Said . . .

If she is "acting out" deferred grief in confrontational or risky ways, focus on talking about her feelings as much as her behavior.

Stacey, I'm not going to fight with you about a slammed door, but I hope you'll apologize for it later. I do want to talk about why we're not getting along well these days. That worries me a lot.

Your attitude obviously has a lot of strong feelings behind it. I have to meet with Grandma right now, but I want you to know that I'm thinking about what you might be feeling, and I want you to tell me about that later.

I'm not sure that we connected very well a few months ago when Granddad died. I was so busy back then trying to get everything done. You and I didn't have much time together. Can we go out to lunch together? I miss you.

Later, after Grandma leaves, let's go to the track and walk. I want you to help me think of ways we might remember Granddad together. I don't think we've taken time to really talk about how much we miss him, and how awful it was for everybody when he died.

"IT'S YOUR FAULT WE'RE BROKE"

Girl: *I got a letter from camp. They have a special two-week "explorers" session this summer. I want to go.*

Mom: *It's probably not in the cards this summer. You know we have to cut back on extras while I'm job hunting.*

Girl: *Yeah, but this is camp—my camp. I go every year.*

Mom: *You know this year is different. We've talked about it before. I don't have money for frills.*

Girl: *Camp is not a frill. Camp is something I need. What am I supposed to do—just sit around all summer?*

Mom: *The money isn't there this year.*

Girl: *This sucks. How did I get stuck with this family? It's your fault we're broke.*

What Just Happened?

As I write this chapter, many families are experiencing hard economic times. This is something new for our daughters, and for many of us. When our girls were little, the United States experienced an economic boom. Many girls grew up being told yes when they asked for things more often than they were told no.

When income falls, everybody in the family is likely to feel deprived. And if we argue over the money we do have, harsh words follow. It may help you to restate the basic values of your family—for example, that you'll continue to take care of each other the best ways you can, no matter how much money you have or don't have.

It may also help to introduce family history into conversations about cutting back. We all have stories about times when our own parents and grandparents met challenges and overcame them.

Each time you tell your daughter these stories, you strengthen her by reminding her that she comes from a long line of people who rose to the occasion during hard times.

Finally, couch cutbacks in terms of "choices"—this gives a girl a sense of power. As you cut back, make sure she has some money over which she has control, and be on the lookout for ways she can earn money of her own (an essential skill for a girl of any age).

What If You Said . . .

If money is an issue, focus your comments on the choices the family must make and restate your basic values.

I can understand why you want to blame somebody, and I'm the most convenient person, but I hope you'll rethink that remark. We'll get through this more easily if we stick together instead of blaming each other for problems we can't prevent.

Let's brainstorm some answers. Go get the camp info, and we'll talk about ways you could earn part of the money, or whether you could get a camp session instead of birthday or holiday gifts this year. Maybe this boils down to choices on your part.

I'm sorry we don't have money for camp this summer. You know, this money bind is probably a temporary problem for us. We'll have better years. In the meantime, what matters most is that we are together and love each other. I know we'd like to have more, but in many ways we're blessed.

This family you're "stuck with" has been through hard times before. Did you know your grandmother didn't have a birthday cake during World War II because sugar was rationed? And she was so worried while Grandpa was off fighting. I'd like to know more about those days myself. Let's call her up and talk to her.

Apologies and Forgiveness

*How can you open the door to apologies—
both the ones you need to make and
the ones you'd like to hear?*

*Reconciliation is typically initiated by me. I say,
"I'm sorry I yelled at you this morning. I was anxious,
and I shouldn't have taken it out on you." Dawne will say
something like, "That's okay, Dad. Don't worry about it."
That's usually all it takes. Then we can talk about something else, like what happened that day. The blowup
typically happens in the morning before school, and the
reconciliation usually comes while fixing dinner that
night. I feel better when it comes with an
"I love you" and a hug.*

—Manuel, father of a 13-year-old girl

*I once told my mom I hated her. I ran up to my room
and cried, and I realized I was acting like a baby just
because I didn't get my way. I never told her I was sorry.
Instead, I went downstairs and told her I loved her. I
think that meant more to her than just saying sorry. But
I would take back what I said in a second if I could. Our
relationship has never been exactly the same since then.*

—EmilyAnne, age 12

When the girls we surveyed described fights with their parents, they talked about the thick of the fight as a release of feeling, an explosion of words. Many girls expressed relief because their emotions had broken out into the open. For example, 14-year-old Carly admitted, "I felt sort of taller after I stood up to my mom." Over and over, girls wrote, "It felt good at the time," with something like guilty glee. Even if the words will need to be taken back later, it can be a great relief to a girl to take control of her space, of her life, of her frustration—with words.

In that moment when my daughter puts her hands on her hips and tells me to get out of her life, she forces me to *see* her, to recognize her, and to deal with her. She simultaneously drives me away with her words *and* compels me into close relationship by demanding my attention. As EmilyAnne notes previously, such moments change things. Nothing between us is ever really exactly the same again.

In the same way you know a competitor better after a game, we and our daughters know each other better after a fight. At some level, a girl who is yelling at you is saying, "This awful behavior is what I am capable of. This is part of me you have not seen before, and you may not like it!" Make no mistake, this is a test. She wants to know if you can bear her words and still somehow maintain the love between you. The answer lies in apologies. At their best, apologies bring us back together and mend what was torn. At their worst, they bury strong feelings that will come back to haunt us. The difference is up to us.

Some girls apologize easily. Generally speaking, women are more comfortable making apologies than men are. Girls work hard to keep their relationships in repair, and they worry less than boys do about retaining the power position in conversations. Indeed, sometimes girls and women apologize for things they had no part in.[1] But that does not mean your daughter will apologize easily to you, at least not all the time.

The Girl's View: "I Have No Power"

In chapter 2, "When Words Hurt," we talked about the factors that send us parents into emotional overdrive when we argue with our daughters. Beyond all that intensity, there are also automatic grievances on both sides. Simply by virtue of being children, girls feel overpowered by us. Adults have power over their lives, and that makes apologizing tough for them. Between the ages of 8 and 12, a girl is struggling to become more self-reliant. During a fight, a parent represents everything that holds her back from independence. As she sees it, *the parent* is her problem. Why should she apologize to her oppressor?

I still remember the frozen, frightened feeling I used to get as a kid after I had a fight with one of my parents. Up in my room, I would cry and plan my strategy for when I saw my mom or dad again. Sometimes my plan was not to speak to my parents ever again. Sometimes the plan was to act as if nothing had happened. It was easier that way. Apologizing to my parents made me feel powerless. Sometimes a girl just cannot bear to go through that,

1. Deborah Tannen, *You Just Don't Understand* (New York: Morrow Avon, 1990).

at least not yet. She reasons that it's better to dry her tears, lift her chin, and make nicey-nice as if nothing ever happened. (And sometimes it works because lots of adults aren't comfortable with apologies either.)

This is why we parents don't always get the apologies we deserve, and why it's so important for us to find words that let girls know it's safe (meaning that we won't make them feel worse than before) to apologize to us.

The Parent's View: "Wait, I Didn't Do All That!"

While girls feel overpowered in a fight, we parents tend to feel overaccused. Adolescent girls—simply because of their developmental stage—tend to overstate our offenses.[2] Sometimes, in the middle of an argument, we find ourselves accused of emotional crimes we never committed. If I speak sharply to my daughter, I may be told that I've ruined not just the moment, but her whole life, thank you very much, and another thing, I criticize her *all* the time and *never* praise her.

It's awfully hard to apologize for my one or two sharp words when I'm being accused of crushing my daughter's self-esteem and devastating all her future prospects for happiness. At a moment like this, I feel like telling her that she doesn't know what a good thing she has in me—but somehow I don't feel like apologizing, not one little bit (even if, okay, I *did* snap at her a little). Apologies are hard to make on both sides. That's why making up between parents and daughters often begins silently, with a glance or a teary smile. Some of the most touching stories parents told me about making up after a fight were not so much about words but about feelings.

2. The idea of being "overaccused" is a concept from Harriet Lerner's *The Dance of Connection* (New York: Harper Collins, 2002).

When it comes to healing things after we've said something disastrous—this is usually accomplished without words. "I'm sorry" or an explanation of why I said what I did usually comes after we've reconnected emotionally, and that is usually done with eye contact followed by a smile followed by a hug. Then we can use words again.

—Mim, mother of a 13-year-old girl

When I've gotten angry with her, I've apologized and tried to let her know that I love her, that I only want what's best for her. I try to engage her and give her a chance to let me know what she's feeling, but usually she is stone silent. Later in the day, or even a day later, she'll warm up. I think we both recognize those moments as points of reconciliation. We just don't always express them directly with words. These moments don't go unnoticed by me, and I'm always touched by them.

—Larry, father of a 12-year-old girl

Apologizing and forgiving means letting go of the emotional hurt and heat of the exchange. Sometimes this happens simply, almost silently. It doesn't take many words to apologize, just the right ones. With feeling, "I'm sorry" speaks volumes.

The Apologies We Remember

The parents and girls we surveyed gave us clues about what kinds of apologies are remembered the longest. These ideas can make your apologies more effective:

Use the evening hours. Time and again, girls reported making apologies "when the sun went down." Even if a girl can keep her anger burning through the day, she may lower her defenses and be open to saying or hearing words of regret in the evening.

State the obvious. Girls remember apologies in which we parents specifically voice our ongoing love. One ten-year-old named Shannon recalled, "My mom told me I was the best girl in the world, and she would never trade me in for anybody else. For the first time in two days she put a smile on my face." Another girl, nine-year-old Heather, quoted her dad word for word: "You are the last person I would want to hurt." Affirmations of this sort take root in our daughters' memories.

Seal the deal. Sometimes we forget that girls think concretely more than they think abstractly. Make a symbolic gesture like taking a walk together, eating a special food together, or going to the movies. This reinforces the apology and assures a girl—especially a preteen—that the relationship is back on track.

"I SAID 'SORRY.' CAN WE MOVE ON?"

Mom: *I want to talk about what happened earlier today. I don't feel right when it's like this and we're angry with each other.*

Girl: *(rolls her eyes) So we'll talk.*

Mom: *I wish I hadn't yelled at you. I remember how awful it feels to have a parent mad at you like that. I'm really sorry.*

Girl: *Me, too. Sorry.*

Mom: *Thanks. I guess we're going to be irritated with each other sometimes, no matter how hard we try.*

Girl: *I guess. Can we move on here? I already said "Sorry!"*

What Just Happened?

Whenever a girl goes through a stage when her identity feels threatened (and that could be any time during her adolescent years), she feels vulnerable expressing regret. And you and I are the hardest people of all for her to apologize to, because we're the very ones she wants to convince of her maturity.

Researchers have observed that, given the opportunity, most school-age girls will repair arguments with a simple "sorry" rather than delving into what went wrong in the first place.[1] They do this with friends, and they do this with parents. In fact, the girls we heard from in our survey often told stories about parent-daughter fights in which, like a magic wand, "sorry" made everything okay.

If your daughter has trouble apologizing to you in a meaningful way, her lack of words may come from having too much feeling rather than too little. As we've noted before, most girls feel completely safe and whole only when their primary relationships are

1. Rachel Simmons, *Odd Girl Out: The Hidden Culture of Aggression in Girls* (New York: Harcourt Trade, 2002).

in place. Therefore, exploring a relational rift in detail can be frightening to a girl. Mumbling "sorry" is lots easier. Use the words below to get past a cursory or insincere "sorry."

What If You Said . . .

Acknowledge how hard it is for your daughter to apologize, help her feel safe, and talk about your need to clear the air of bad feelings.

I'm grateful you said you're sorry. Apologizing is hard. It can make everything seem worse before it makes you feel better.

Later, when we have a little distance from this, let's talk about what happened and how it felt to both of us. I'm not going to hound you about what went wrong—I just love you so much that I don't want us to fight like that. I want to understand what happened.

I know it's hard for you to apologize to me, and I was listening when you said you were sorry. Thanks for having the courage to say that. In fact, it takes a lot of maturity.

I'm not sure I understand what happened between us. If you'll tell me your side of it without yelling, I'll listen without interrupting. Once we clear the air, we can move on and forgive each other completely. I love you so much. I don't want the memory of this fight hanging around to hurt us later on.

"DON'T 'HI, MOM' ME!"

Girl: *(two hours after blowup with Mom) Hi, Mom. What's for dinner?*

Mom: *(looking up with a frown) Spaghetti.*

Girl: *I'll set the table. I heard the phone ring. Who called?*

Mom: *Will you stop it? I can't believe you'd just waltz in here and 'Hi, Mom' me after the things you said earlier! Do you think I've forgotten? You can't treat people like that and then expect them to just forget about it!*

What Just Happened?

What should you do when you deserve an apology, but there's no sign that one is coming? This is one of those times when we have to remember how threatened our daughters often feel when they apologize. Remind yourself, again, that you are the adult and that your adolescent daughter is still a kid. If she is a girl who eventually comes around, your best move may be simply to wait.

> *I've grown up some myself over the last few years and I'm more careful than I've ever been to just back down and let Liz cool off. When I do this, she has time to collect herself and think things through, and it's then that she'll let me know—with a request or an unrelated good-natured jab— that we're okay again. My behavior doesn't change then. I'm just glad to see her back.*
>
> —Tim, father of a 12-year-old girl

You and I will not get an apology from a girl every time we deserve one, and, as Tim's story illustrates, we may not need a verbal one. If your daughter has cut you with harsh comments, however, you do her no favors by ignoring the power of those words.

Try to state your desire for an apology only once. She will hear you. By asking several times or seeming to beg for an apology, you put more responsibility and power in a girl's hands than she, a kid, can really handle. While you want her to know you would appreciate an apology, you do not want to give her the false impression that you are at her mercy.

What If You Said . . .

If she ignores the need to apologize, state your needs clearly and simply. Then let her be. If you need to vent your feelings, confide in other adults. As parents, we cannot force an apology from a child, but we can create a setting in which she feels safe offering one.

We can't ignore the fight we had. Your words do have consequences, and I hope that in time you'll apologize for what you said. But it was just one fight, and that's all it was. We have years of good memories, too. I love you very much.

I don't think it will help if we try to ignore what happened. When you feel ready to talk about the fight, I'll be ready to listen. I love you, do you know that? Now set the table.

Your words were hurtful, and I'd like to hear an apology. But I know it's hard to apologize, and you probably feel hurt, too. When you're ready, I'd like to talk about all that.

"I DON'T KNOW IF I CAN EVER FORGIVE MYSELF!"

Mom: *(an hour after saying something hurtful to daughter)*
I can't believe I said that to you. Can you ever forgive me,
honey? Do you hate me now?

Girl: *No, you just lost it, but now it's over. Don't make such a big*
deal about it, Mom.

Mom: *I was just so upset about your brother. I was distracted and*
wasn't thinking about what I was saying to you. It was a hard
day at work, and now this! I am so, so sorry. I don't feel like
much of a mom when I do something like that.

Girl: *Really, Mom. That's enough. I said it was okay.*

Mom: *Please say you forgive me.*

What Just Happened?

An apology should be about the person who was hurt. A true apology is a gift, not a request. It doesn't burden the other person with your problems, your excuses, or your need to be forgiven. In the example above, the mom seems to have rushed into her apology without taking time to process what happened and to forgive herself first. As a result, she demands understanding and forgiveness from her daughter, instead of providing the girl relief from her hurt. She has made the apology about herself rather than about easing her daughter's pain.

When you apologize, just apologize. Don't make excuses, explain, or ask your daughter to forgive you (that will be her choice). Carefully listen to her story of what happened, without interrupting. Acknowledge her feelings and your own. Finally, express your regret. There's nothing sweeter than a clean, unencumbered apology.

What If You Said . . .

When you apologize in a way that recognizes the pain you caused without demanding anything in return, you set an example your daughter will follow when she needs to apologize to you.

I am so sorry this happened between us. I'm sorry I caused you pain.

I feel very sorry for what I said. I love you so much. You take up a big space in my heart, and you always will.

I want to be able to apologize to you, but first I have to understand more about what happened. Can you tell me your side of it from the beginning? I'll try not to interrupt, though if I get upset, I might need to take a break. Is that okay?

An Apology That Works

When Mariah Burton Nelson examines apologies in The Unburdened Heart *(HarperCollins 2000), she concludes that an effective apology addresses three things:*

What happened (admitting that someone got hurt)

How it felt (showing compassion for the other person)

Taking responsibility (saying, "I'm sorry. I was wrong.")

The step we often skip is the second one. But without it, an "I'm sorry" can really mean, "That's done. Be quiet about it." Then the bad feelings linger. Developing empathy for the other person involved is the beginning of forgiveness.

"I DON'T NEED TO APOLOGIZE—YOU DO!"

Mom: *I heard what you called me when I turned my back. That was very disrespectful. I need an apology.*

Girl: *What I called you? I didn't call you anything. You must be hearing voices.*

Mom: *(calmly) I don't think so.*

Girl: *I don't owe you any kind of apology. But you owe me one— big-time. You never do half the stuff you say you will. You forgot my piano lesson—again! What kind of mother is that?*

Mom: *Obviously a better one than you deserve right now.*

Girl: *Well, if I'm so bad, whose fault is that?*

What Just Happened?

The mom in this scenario is doing a great job of keeping her cool as her daughter baits her. She deserves an apology, but her daughter is on the attack instead. Even with good kids, there are hard times. Sometimes girls say whatever they can to hurt us and make us feel guilty or fearful. Reasons behind these attacks vary, but often a girl who does this feels a need to control the world around her—including you. At a time like this, she's not going to meet you halfway and make (or even accept) an apology.

Here's a wonderful little secret. You don't have to *like* your daughter when she does this sort of thing. Don't let anybody tell you otherwise. Of course, you'll continue to love her and believe in her—that's different—but we don't do our daughters any favors by making excuses for their behavior and allowing them to manipulate or hurt us.

Most girls try out a little manipulation on us now and then, just to see if it will work. It's part of growing up. As babies, they have to be the center of our attention; otherwise they literally might die. As they get older, they resist giving up center stage. Some girls will provoke us no end to make sure we're still noticing them.

If that happens—and especially if it happens often—do what the mom in our dialogue above is doing. Stay firm and don't get into a power struggle. Tell your daughter you won't play this game, and remind yourself not to shout. Shouting lets her know that you're losing control.

What If You Said . . .

Use a calm voice (even if you have to fake it), and tell your daughter you aren't going to cooperate with her tactics.

This isn't about what kind of parent I am. This is about the language you used.

I can see that you're finding ways to avoid your responsibility for what you said to me. It doesn't work, you know, to strike out like this. It just drives people away.

Let's not do this. I'm going to do us both a favor and end the conversation. Try sending me some e-mail. Maybe writing down your thoughts will help you sort things out.

This won't work. I'm not going to fight with you about this. When you are ready to talk with me about what's really going on, I'll listen. But I won't listen to this.

"I'M SORRY THAT YOU FEEL OFFENDED"

Mom: *An apology from you would be appropriate right now. It would help me feel better about what happened between us.*

Girl: *Okay, I guess I'm sorry for whatever I did.*

Mom: *Why do I feel as if you didn't apologize?*

Girl: *Okay then! If you felt offended by what I said, I'm sorry you felt that way.*

What Just Happened?

We've all encountered non-apologetic apologies—the ones that turn aside guilt and responsibility like Teflon. Sometimes we hear them from a daughter. Her words come out, and "sorry" is in there somewhere, but she takes no responsibility for the hurt she caused or the mistake she made. Sometimes non-apologies show up when a girl feels she must maintain a "good girl" image—both to herself and to those around her. But any kid who is feeling particularly ashamed or unduly criticized is likely to fall back on a non-apology.

If your daughter does this only occasionally, the particular situation may be the cause. Perhaps this is a case in which she actually feels she's in the right, but telling you that would be too confrontational or difficult. If you notice a pattern of non-apologies, though, you'll want to explore what's going on. Ask what insecurity or fear might cause your daughter to have to keep feelings of guilt at bay. Sometimes kids who won't apologize feel extremely guilty or unworthy down deep, and they fear that one sincere apology would open the floodgates and reveal everything.

Your best move is probably to acknowledge the pain apologizing causes for your daughter. It is usually a mistake to make too big a deal about non-apologies. In doing so, we add to a girl's guilty feelings, and we add one more grievance to the list of things we already fight with her about. Instead, speak honestly about non-apologies when you hear them, and model sincere apologies and self-acceptance yourself. Each time your daughter sees you admit fault without debilitating self-blame, she becomes more likely to learn this skill for herself.

What If You Said . . .

Real apologies can't be forced. Respect your daughter's inability to apologize, and don't insist on a sincere apology. If she appears to be struggling with some guilt, affirm her basic goodness. That will help her feel less threatened by apologies.

I don't think that was an apology. Maybe you feel that you have to protect yourself right now. I can understand that if it's true.

I can see you aren't comfortable apologizing about this. If you find the words to really apologize sometime soon, I'd appreciate hearing them.

We all make mistakes, so we all have to apologize. It's hard to do. I know that myself. It's painful to admit you did something wrong.

I know that you're a good kid. I see that in you every day. No matter what you do wrong and have to apologize for, I'll always know that about you—that you have a good, good heart.

If there's a pattern of non-apologies:

I hope you know that no matter what you do, I will always love you. And I know that someday soon, you'll act more responsibly than you're acting right now.

A Final Note
You know the "right" words
when they come to you.

A s I've contemplated these stories over the past months, there have been times when I felt like the little Dutch boy with his finger in the dike, holding a tall, watery wall at bay. That's what it's like when we're looking for words to say when we're in conflict with our daughters. In the heat or sadness of that moment, even the "right" words feel inadequate, unable to convey the immense feelings that flood our hearts. And yet, words matter so.

Who knows what the "right" words will be at your house? One mother told me about the hardest words she'd ever said to her daughter. After a long period of extreme turmoil, she and her husband decided to be very firm with their daughter, who was 11 years old at the time. They said, "You have no rights. From now on, every right and privilege you have has to be earned." Today, this daughter recalls how that conversation changed everything, reframing her relationship with her parents and giving them all a new start.

In contrast, a dad told me about years of being insensitive to his daughters' feelings, just as his parents had been dismissive of his feelings as a child. His path to rebuilding his relationships with his daughters began with the words, "You have the right to be angry at me. You have the right to be listened to . . ."

Such different words. Yet in each case, words created a new relationship when the old one was broken. That is what words do—they let us start over.

Resource Guide

The following books can help you understand the ups and downs of communicating with your daughter, improve your own communication skills, and strengthen your parent-daughter relationship for the long term.

The Dance of Connection by Harriet Lerner (New York: HarperCollins, 2002). Lerner's books explore the dynamics of relationships—mostly adult relationships—but contain insight about how we relate to children, too. With powerful stories and practical advice, *The Dance of Connection* emphasizes how we use our voices to express our connections and needs.

Emotional Intelligence: Why It Can Matter More than IQ by Daniel Goleman (New York: Bantam Books, 1996). The seminal book that defined "emotional intelligence" as a critical set of skills that allow us to identify and share our feelings, build relationships with others, and set and achieve goals.

Father Courage: What Happens When Men Put Family First by Suzanne Braun Levine (New York: Harcourt Press, 2000). This book is a must-read for any dad trying to achieve success at work and stay connected to his daughter at the same time.

Levine offers insight into the conflict and pressures dads feel and solutions that can help.

Fathering: Strengthening Connection with Your Children No Matter Where You Are by Will Glennon (Boston: Conari Press, 1995). This perennial favorite is a great read for any dad who feels he has lost touch with his children. Glennon offers stories of hope and ideas you can use.

The First Sex: The Natural Talents of Women and How They Are Changing the World by Helen Fisher (New York: Ballantine Books, 2000). Research about gender-driven communication skills and the advantages they give girls and women.

Games Girls Play: Understanding and Guiding Young Female Athletes by Caroline Silby and Shelley Smith (New York: St. Martin's Press, 2000). Advice that can help any parent support an active girl, with specific ideas for talking about nervousness before sporting events, losses, and advice regarding social and physical problems related to sports.

A General Theory of Love by Thomas Lewis, Fari Amini, and Richard Lannon (New York: Vintage, 2001). A survey of what science has learned about how emotional resonance works, what it means to feel love or be loved, and how a child's sense of self is shaped by her parents.

Girl in the Mirror: Mothers and Daughters in the Years of Adolescence by Nancy Snyderman and Peg Streep (New York: Hyperion Press, 2002). This book explores the evolution of a mom's developing sense of self as she enters new stages of her life and her daughter's corresponding development. While this book is not about words per se, it offers insight and understanding into the reasons we struggle to adapt to each other's constantly changing identities.

Girls Will Be Girls: Raising Courageous and Confident Daughters by JoAnn Deak (New York: Hyperion Press, 2002). An educator who understands what girls need in order to thrive, Deak turns the old girls-as-victims adage on its ear, writing eloquently about the ways we can foster healthy risk taking in girls by recognizing and encouraging

their innate strengths, including their voices.

How to Mother a Successful Daughter (New York: Harmony Books, 1999) and *How to Father a Successful Daughter* (New York: Fawcett, 1999), both by Nicky Marone. With advice for moms and for dads, Marone provides powerful and practical words we can use (including visualizations and affirmations) to help our daughters become self-confident and resilient.

"I'm Not Mad, I Just Hate You!": A New Understanding of Mother-Daughter Conflict by Roni Cohen-Sandler (New York: Penguin Putnam, 2000). A basic understanding of the psychology behind mom-daughter conflict, including insight into how the things that were said to us by our parents affect what we say to our daughters today.

Nourishing Your Daughter: Help Your Child Develop a Healthy Relationship with Food and Her Body by Carol Beck (New York: Perigee, 2001). Beck emphasizes the feelings behind eating behaviors, and she includes helpful sections called "healthy responses" in her text, words that can help us avoid fighting about food.

Raising Emotionally Intelligent Teenagers: Guiding the Way for

Compassionate, Committed, Courageous Adults by Maurice Elias, Steven Tobias, and Brian Friedlander (New York: Three Rivers Press, 2002). Excellent advice about communicating in an empathetic and caring way as a parent, at the same time you're setting limits and teaching your daughter to be responsible. The authors make good use of humor and offer sample dialogues and insight into body language.

Rituals for Our Times: Celebrating, Healing, and Changing Our Lives and Our Relationships by Evan Imber-Black and Janine Roberts (New York: HarperCollins, 1992). An excellent guide to creating words and actions that honor changing relationships.

Strong, Smart & Bold: Empowering Girls for Life by Carla Fine (New York: HarperCollins, 2001). Based on the powerful principles of Girls, Inc., this books explores the real-life skills girls need to take care of themselves in the real world. Among those skills is "Speaking Freely and Openly"—a chapter that will help you hear words from your daughter's point of view.

What I Wish You Knew: Letters from Our Daughters' Lives, and Expert Advice on Staying Connected by the editors of

American Girl (Pleasant Company Publications, 2001). Letters written to American Girl relate the issues on the minds of girls ages 10 to 14. Psychologists who specialize in girls' issues provide advice and insight into each letter. Offers practical ways to talk about tough subjects like girls' changing bodies, struggles with friends, stress, speaking up, dating, and experimenting with drugs and alcohol.

Will You Still Love Me If I Don't Win?: A Guide for Parents of Young Athletes by Christopher Andersonn (Owatonna, MN: Taylor Publishing, 2000). Insight into the emotions we feel when our daughters win and lose, and how those feelings shape the words we say and the bonds we form with our daughters.

You Just Don't Understand: Women and Men in Conversation by Deborah Tannen (New York: Quill, 2001). The classic book about how women and men (and girls and boys) use language in distinctly different ways. There are insights here about why your daughter is likely to talk in certain situations but clam up in others, about the body language she uses, and about the many ways she is likely to use words to connect rather than to compete.

Editions listed are the most current available.

Index

Expert Advice for Parents
from the editors of American Girl ®

From the creators of trusted advice books for girls comes an
insightful and eloquent guide for parents. *What I Wish You Knew*
combines girls' letters with expert advice from psychologists and
educators specializing in girls' issues. Parents will learn practical,
real-life ways to talk with their daughters about important subjects,
support them through difficult times, and create strong bonds
with them that will last a lifetime. 226 pages. $12.95

*"A lively, informative guide to the land of adolescent girls. This book should
make for honest and healing discussions."*

—Mary Pipher, author of *Reviving Ophelia*

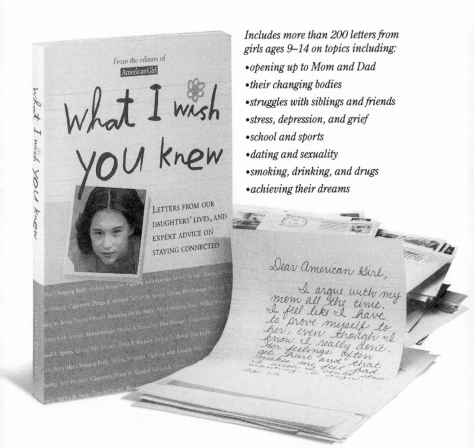

*Includes more than 200 letters from
girls ages 9–14 on topics including:*

- *opening up to Mom and Dad*
- *their changing bodies*
- *struggles with siblings and friends*
- *stress, depression, and grief*
- *school and sports*
- *dating and sexuality*
- *smoking, drinking, and drugs*
- *achieving their dreams*

For more information, visit your local bookstore or **americangirl.com**

Help your daughter help herself with advice books from American Girl Library®, written specifically for girls ages 8 to 12.

The Feelings Book: The Care & Keeping of Your Emotions. This companion to the popular *The Care & Keeping of You* helps girls understand and deal with their ever-changing emotions. It teaches girls how to express their feelings and stay in control, plus gives sensitive advice on handling fear, anxiety, jealousy, and grief. 104 pages. $8.95

The Care & Keeping of You: The Body Book for Girls. This head-to-toe guide answers all your daughter's questions, from hair care to healthy eating, bad breath to bras, periods to pimples. A national bestseller. 114 pages. $9.95

The Care & Keeping of Me. An interactive companion journal to *The Care & Keeping of You.* Includes a

period tracker and mood recorder, plus tips, quizzes, and checklists to help girls keep in touch with their changing bodies. 96 pages. $7.95

The Smart Girl's Guide to Boys: Surviving Crushes, Staying True to Yourself, and Other Love Stuff. Caring advice on how girls can feel good and be themselves around boys. Letters, tips, and quizzes cover how to talk to a boy, what to do if her friends like boys and she doesn't, and dealing with rejection. 112 pages. $9.95

Help! A Girl's Guide to Divorce and Stepfamilies. When a girl's parents break up, her world can turn upside down. American Girl answers letters on every aspect of divorce, from the initial split to a parent's remarriage. Includes tips, quizzes, and advice from girls who've been there. Parents Choice award and National Parenting Publications award winner. 128 pages. $8.95

Staying Home Alone: A Girl's Guide to Staying Safe and Having Fun. Packed with safety tips, recipes, quizzes, and fun-for-one ideas, this book helps girls keep their cool when they're on their own. Includes advice on battling boredom and getting along with siblings, plus contact lists to tear out and fill in. 72 pages. $7.95

A Smart Girl's Guide to Friendship Troubles: Dealing with Fights, Being Left Out, and the Whole Popularity Thing. How can she speak up without hurting her friend's feelings? What if her friend leaves her for a more popular crowd? And when—or how—does she get Mom or Dad involved? Quizzes and real stories from girls round out this advice-packed book. 86 pages. $9.95.

Yikes! A Smart Girl's Guide to Surviving Tricky, Sticky, Icky Situations. Problem-solving strategies and tips help girls take charge and feel confident in tough situations—from being bullied to getting caught in an earthquake to falling down the stairs at school. Appropriate for children ages 10 and over. 88 pages. $8.95

I Can Do Anything! This colorful book of inspirations features 32 tear-out cards that combine bold graphics with encouraging words like "What I think matters!" and "Mean what you say, say what you mean, but don't say it mean." Topics include

being yourself and dealing with competition, anger, and sadness. Ready to be taped up on the wall or shared with a friend. 66 pages. $6.95

Oh, Brother . . . Oh, Sister! A Sister's Guide to Getting Along. Having a brother or sister (or several!) can be both a joy and a pain. Here's practical advice on issues brothers and sisters face, including fighting, sharing, jealousy, and respect. Tips and quizzes help make family life easier. 64 pages. $7.95

Good Sports: Winning. Losing. And Everything in Between. This spirited advice book helps girls feel strong and sure of them-selves on the basketball court, soccer field, or wherever they like to play. Includes tips on dealing with jitters and taking charge when the going gets tough. The message? Run fast, play hard, and have fun! Parents Choice award winner. 96 pages. $8.95

Oops! The Manners Guide for Girls. What's that funny fork for? How should a girl say "thank you" for a gift she doesn't like? Girls can find out in this introduction to the social skills they need to navigate life with grace and confidence. 116 pages. $7.95

For more information, visit your local bookstore or **americangirl.com**

About the Authors

AMY LYNCH writes about the lives of girls and women. She was the founding editor of *Daughters* newsletter, a resource for the parents of adolescent girls, and is publisher of *OurSelves,* the newsletter for women at the center of life. Her articles have appeared in *Ms., First for Women, Inc.,* and other national publications, and she was editorial consultant for the award-winning Pleasant Company book, *What I Wish You Knew: Letters from Our Daughters' Lives, and Expert Advice on Staying Connected.*

Lynch is the mom of two outspoken daughters, and she has been known to speak her mind from time to time herself. (Her husband, thank goodness, is the quiet type.) When she is not having "frank" discussions at home, she speaks to parent groups and other organizations about helping girls grow up strong. Lynch lives in Nashville, Tennessee, and can be reached at amy-lynch@ourselves.com

LINDA G. ASHFORD, Ph.D., is a psychologist on the pediatrics faculty at Vanderbilt University Medical Center in Nashville, Tennessee. She works with children and families in a clinic setting, teaches psychology at Peabody College of Vanderbilt University, and has written on the subject of parenting girls. She is the mother of two daughters and lives in Nashville with her husband. She enjoys traveling, reading, and the out-of-doors.